Advance Praise for *Share of Culture*

"Paul Parton brilliantly captures what every modern marketer needs to understand: In today's attention economy, the brands that win are those that earn their audience rather than buying it. This book is the definitive playbook for building popularity through authentic storytelling."

—**Matt Neale**, CEO, Golin

"This incredibly well researched tome cuts through the marketing noise with wit and interest. The author tackles some eternal questions about what drives success for brands with a refreshingly modern take. Complex concepts are well studied and explained with care. Prepare to rethink how you build winning brands."

—**Alex Moulle-Berteaux**, CEO, Starry Internet

"For over a decade, I've watched Paul turn brands into market leaders using the unstoppable force of earned-first thinking. Now, he reveals the playbook—every insight, every strategy—for marketers ready to smash declining response rates and build culture-first brands that win"

—**Jackie Stevenson**, Chief Strategy and Innovation Officer, M&C Saatchi

"Paul Parton has taken his native intellect as an advocate for the advancement of marketing, while working in the self-same industry. In doing that he is not a whistle-blower, but a supporter and a savior all at once. More than adapting to the future he is making the future that will sustain marketing as it seeks to adapt to a new set of operating realities. He will need no applause sign."

—**Dr. Bob Deutsch**, Author, *The 5 Essentials: Using Your Inborn Resources to Create a Fulfilling Life*

"Pay attention to Paul Parton! He's got the goods that can rescue marketing from its sad slump of short-termism. This book is a blueprint for building brands that *real* people *really* value. Parton shares his well-earned wisdom with a clarity and charm that has produced a rare gem: a marketing book that is as enjoyable to read as it is useful to own."

—**Michael Fanuele**, Author, *Stop Making Sense: The Art of Inspiring Anybody*

"*Share of Culture* captures the shift every modern marketer senses but few can articulate: that in today's landscape, attention is the true currency, and cultural relevance is the only sustainable advantage. Paul offers a sharp, practical guide to moving from messaging at people to engaging with them. A timely and essential read."

—**Kamran Asghar**, Founder and CEO, Crossmedia

"It's been twenty years since *Ad Age* columnist Bob Garfield's dystopian *The Chaos Scenario* painted a bleak future for the ad industry, and Paul Parton picks up where the tipping point left off in his new book *Share of Culture*. Not surprisingly, the agency insider and consumer marketing expert finds things have only gotten worse due to the acceleration of digital media, the influx of a multitude of new brands, messages, and communications options, and a dramatic shift from the practice of long-term brand building equity to short term performance marketing results. While Parton doesn't paint a very pretty picture, he sets the groundwork for a new organizing principle for modern marketing. Actually, two of them: knowing the "truth of your brand" and live by it; and getting people talking about it. That might sound easier said than done, but *Share of Culture* provides numerous, successful real-world examples from recent history, as well some guideposts for where the marketing hockey puck will be heading next. More than anything, Parton's book provides concrete ways for brands to reorient and adapt to a continuously changing world of consumer marketing by identifying what works, and what no longer does."

—**Joe Mandese**, Editor in Chief, Mediapost

"Today, marketing is everywhere but, at the same time, it's almost invisible. We are bombarded by millions of ads, but most of them do not really land. Paul Parton's *Share of Culture* really uncovers why effective marketing is more difficult to identify. For someone like me, who leads a company that is driven by our purpose, his take on things really hits home.

"Companies are throwing so much money at short-term ads that just fizzle out, instead of building something lasting. Efforts to try to be everything to everyone just makes us forget who we are as brands. He calls it the 'Achilles' heel of modern marketing,' and he's not wrong.

"We all know the media has changed—audiences are shrinking, and people are just plain tired of ads. So, we're paying more to reach fewer people, which is just crazy.

Paul does a great job of underscoring that in this 'attention economy' (where attention is gold), being real and authentic is the absolute best way to stand out. If you are clear about your brand's purpose and what you believe in, that's what truly connects with people.

"His real-world examples (Glossier, Tesla, and K-Pop sensation BTS) share very different approaches to effective marketing, noting the common denominator is being authentic. Paul's use of the Oscar Wilde quote sums it up perfectly: 'Be yourself; everyone else is already taken.'

"So if you're in marketing, or you run a business, or you just want to understand how to actually connect with people today, you *have* to read this. *Share of Culture* is a wake-up call to ditch the old, generic stuff and really figure out your brand's true identity. It's all about building real connections, getting people talking, and inviting them to be part of something. Paul perfectly lands the idea that in a world where everyone's trying to grab attention, being truly, authentically *you* is the biggest win there is."

—**Noel Wallace**, CEO and Chair,
The Colgate-Palmolive Company

SHARE
OF
CULTURE

HOW BRANDS GROW IN
THE ATTENTION ECONOMY

PAUL PARTON

Post Hill
PRESS

A POST HILL PRESS BOOK
ISBN: 979-8-89565-433-0
ISBN (eBook): 979-8-89565-434-7

Cover design by Conroy Accord

This is a work of nonfiction. All people, locations, events, and situations are portrayed to the best of the author's memory.

Although every effort has been made to ensure that the personal and professional advice present within this book is useful and appropriate, the author and publisher do not assume and hereby disclaim any liability to any person, business, or organization choosing to employ the guidance offered in this book.

This book, as well as any other Post Hill Press publications, may be purchased in bulk quantities at a special discounted rate. Contact orders@posthillpress.com for more information.

Post Hill Press
New York • Nashville
posthillpress.com

Published in the United States of America
1 2 3 4 5 6 7 8 9 10

CONTENTS

PART THREE
A New Marketing Model

PART FOUR
Applying the Model

PART FIVE
Evaluating the Effect

INTRODUCTION

Marketing isn't working. And it's been on life support for years.

Just to be clear, that isn't an attempt to raise ire, fan flames, or cause outrage. It's a statement of fact. It is empirical. There has been a measurable reduction in marketing performance that's been getting worse for a dozen years.

The irony here is that those dozen years have also been marked by the meteoric rise of performance marketing, digital media, precision targeting, and a fixation on measuring the short-term impact of marketing—all of which implicitly promise an immediate improvement in marketing impact and efficiency.

And that is the problem.

The simple, inalienable truth about marketing is that it is made up of a yin and a yang: the yin of the short term and the yang of the long term. Alternatively stated, the yin of performance marketing and the yang of brand building.

Performance marketing is short term. It is the process of making your product the most likely to be bought at exactly the moment that someone needs it. It is the process of getting your brand to the top of the search list. Ensuring that digital ads for waterproof boots appear everywhere you look, directly after you have searched for waterproof boots. It is the direct mail you get from Publishers Clearing House. The holiday catalogs from L.L. Bean. It is the barrage of emails you get about new releases from companies you have bought from before. It is the algorithm that suggests, "You may also like…." It's the reason you see ads on social media for dress shirts after you mentioned to your wife in the car that you might need a new dress shirt. (Hmmm, are they listening?) Some of it is annoying, some of it is intrusive, much of it is effective. All of it is short term. It is also direct, concrete, and measurable, which is very appealing to many marketers.

Brand building, on the other hand, is slightly abstract, somewhat intangible, and focused on the long term. Brand building is the association of images, words, and feelings to a logo, a name, or a symbol. It's why an engagement ring in a Tiffany box feels more valuable than the same ring in a Macy's box. It's why you're reluctant to buy Prada bags in Chinatown. It's why Logan Paul got paid $8.6 million to fight Tommy Fury even though both are terrible boxers. It's why the media continues to fixate on Donald Trump. Brand building is subtle. It requires the same stories to be told and associated with the same set of imagery over a long period of time. Its effects are difficult to predict and difficult to measure.

Within the solar system of commerce, they are entirely different worlds—made up of different people, with different marketing languages, and different goals. Often, the two groups don't understand each other. Often, they don't work together. They're like two different cultures, staring at each other over a common border, scratching their heads in wonder at why the other group speaks funny and wears different clothes.

But one without the other doesn't work.

Brand building without performance marketing creates something lovable and popular that doesn't sell. And performance marketing without brand building creates short-term sales with an inevitable decay in those sales over time.

Which is what has happened to modern marketing. We're creating precise, measurable marketing programs that aren't building popular, famous, lovable brands.

We find ourselves in a situation where the quarter-by-quarter short-termism of the global economy, paired with the intoxicating ability to accurately measure the performance of digital media, has left marketing out of kilter. We're off balance. We're more yin than yang.

Now, the ideal balance between performance marketing and brand building has been studied and boiled down to a simple formula: a marketer should be spending 60 percent of their budget on long-term brand building and 40 percent on short-term performance marketing.

So, why doesn't everyone just do that? Well, therein lies the rub.

Because right now, the equation is almost completely upside down. Marketers are spending 65 percent of their budgets on the short-term, leaving only 35 percent for long-term brand building. And the effect is predictable: a measurable decline in marketing effectiveness over time.

So, what's the solution? Surely, it's as simple as rebalancing the books—moving money from one side of the ledger to the other. Well, not really.

One thing is very clear: very few marketers will reduce their performance media budgets in favor of long-term brand building. They can't! As certain as death and taxes is the fact that Google must be paid. Amazon must be paid. The shopping cart on their website must be optimized. That money is spent. And it would take Herculean strength of will for a CMO to turn to her board and declare that they are going to take a third of their "predictable" performance marketing budget and allocate it to the intangible business of building the brand.

So, if they can't spend more on brand building, can they make their brand building more efficient? Well, yes and no.

Let's start with the negative. No, they can't make their traditional brand-building efforts more efficient. In fact, the modern media marketplace is conspiring to make those efforts materially less efficient. As media audiences are getting smaller, the cost to reach those audiences using traditional brand-building techniques like advertising and sponsorship is getting much higher. In fact, brands are being squeezed between the costs of performance marketing on one hand and the costs of traditional brand-building approaches on the other.

And, then again, yes—there are brands that have been able to make their brand building more efficient. That have managed to thread the needle between long-term brand building and short-term performance.

The same dozen years that witnessed the decline in marketing effectiveness for traditional brands saw the emergence of a new crop of (mainly) direct-to-consumer brands that built their businesses in very different ways, with different expectations, and different operating models.

Many of the brands developed in those years are changing the way we shop, and often, they are changing the way we live. Brands like Glossier, Warby Parker, and Casper are promising to make us more beautiful, to see better, and to sleep better. Others, like Uber, Airbnb, and Tesla, are redefining our consumer infrastructure. We move around cities differently now than we did ten years ago. We vacation differently. We get our groceries and plan our meals differently. We fuel our cars differently.

We take these brands completely for granted now. They are parts of our consumer lives, like American Airlines and Walmart have been for decades. And yet, few of these modern brands are more than twelve years old.

In that short amount of time, these companies haven't just built large and successful businesses; they have built powerful and evocative brands—brands that we trust, that we like, that we admire, and, often, that we aspire to own.

The categories they compete in are wildly different. But there are real commonalities in the way they approach business and brand building. First among them is that these companies were the first generation of digitally native marketers. They grew up in a digital environment and weren't hampered by the legacy of traditional marketing. So, they intuitively mastered the performance marketing that the digital realm offered. And they spent much of their marketing budget on it.

But they still managed to build distinctive and engaging brands. They just did it without relying on traditional marketing techniques—particularly the kind of broadcast-based advertising that most traditional consumer brands have anchored their marketing efforts with for the past seventy years. Instead, they built their brands in new ways using new tools and new techniques.

And those techniques can be boiled down to two simple principles of modern marketing.

Be true to yourself.

Get people talking.

The first principle creates a powerful alchemy that happens when the brand uncovers a truth about itself that also reflects how its audience feels about themselves. This is something the brand believes in that also makes the people they are trying to reach feel seen and feel better about themselves; bigger, more connected, and perhaps less alone. (That they, like Nike, have a competitive spirit that burns inside them, or that they, like President Trump, can make America great again, for example.) Once that central truth is uncovered, the brand declares it to the world. Their beliefs as an organization are clear, and their promise to their customers is succinct. They fly their flag and invite others to fly it with them. They look the part, and they play the part. Their logos are elegant and memorable, and their design language is consistent. They have a clear story to tell the world. They show up in the same way every time we encounter them. They design the experience that surrounds the brand. They design rituals that make it easy to connect to the brand, that are easy to participate in and fun to play with. And they design their narrative, and their sound-bites, so even when the brand is referenced without its logo, it is still recognizable through its words and its actions.

Then, they give people something to talk about. They dance like no one's watching. They are provocative. They do fun, interesting things that people want to write about, and tweet about, and share. They tell their brand story with organic content marketing. They use community management not just to chat with their customers but to inspire product development. They maintain a direct link to popular culture with expert media relations. They create delightful customer moments with experiential marketing. They connect media-friendly social impact to their brand beliefs. They use effective employee communications to empower their workforce. They nurture their community and fuel their fans. They make themselves famous by being entertaining, newsworthy, and always talkable.

And it's not just brands (in the traditional sense) that have benefited from this new form of marketing. In fact, some of the most impactful and impressive cultural, social, and political success stories in the last fifteen years have applied the same techniques for success. From politicians to musicians, TV personalities to social movements, the most successful have executed the same plays from the same playbook.

From Obama's victory in 2008 to Trump's upset in 2016 and his reemergence in 2024. From the recreation of late-night TV to the reinvention of the hospitality industry. From Black Lives Matter to the Boogaloo Boys. Bieber to BTS. All of them were clear about their brand's truth, their purpose, and their role in the world. All of them had a well-defined and memorable image and an engaging and inviting brand experience. And all of them learned how to manipulate the media—both traditional and social—to fuel their popularity. How much media attention would their words, ideas, or actions generate? Who would write about it? Which TV network would pick up the story? How many people would share the video? Who would retweet it? How many memes would it spawn?

That combination of a clearly articulated and memorable brand image, a brand experience that is easy to participate in, and activities that are provocative, entertaining, and interesting enough for people to talk about creates a powerful brand-building effect. The impact of many people simultaneously liking, sharing, commenting on, or writing about the same thing creates a powerful energy around a brand that is appealing. And the ability to harness that conversational energy across social media platforms, podcasts, product forums, group chats, influencer channels, and traditional media has become an enviable skill. And that powerful effect can be deployed for a fraction of the cost that businesses have traditionally paid to build their brands (allowing them to spend their precious marketing budgets on performance media).

What these modern brands and cultural sensations stumbled upon was the realization that if they focused on how they could earn media attention, they could avoid buying media space. And what seemed like overnight, one of the primary barriers to entry for any new player in any cultural sphere was removed. Massive advertising budgets had been the keys to the castle of scale and influence for the last seventy years of the broadcast era. But now, whole categories were being upended by people without access to those advertising war chests. Political establishments were dismantled, businesses were disrupted, and entertainers entertained us in more ways.

Did I say stumble? They didn't really stumble upon anything. These modern marketers were astute and instinctive readers of a media environment that changed almost beyond recognition in a very short space of time.

The digital reinvention of our marketing and media ecosystem created both a perfect storm for traditional marketers and a massive prize for modern marketers. As consumers, we spend more time than ever before with different forms of media. And yet ad-free services, skip buttons, and DVR time-shifting have made it easier than ever to avoid advertising messages. Streaming services (Netflix, Hulu, Prime) allowed people to cut the cord from their cable provider, leaving fewer people watching advertiser-supported broadcast and cable networks. And as audiences for traditional media got smaller, the cost of buying traditional media to reach those audiences got larger—an issue compounded by the transactional taxes paid by marketers to compete in a digital environment (SEO costs, placement fees to Amazon, web optimization costs), which now come out of a marketing budget that used to focus on brand-building activities.

To the new digitally native marketers, it didn't matter. They had found new ways to build fame for their brands. Less expensive paths to popularity. But whereas traditional marketers quickly adopted the performance marketing tricks of their digital competitors, they have been slow to recalibrate their brand-building approaches.

For the last seventy years—since the 1950s—marketers have anchored their brand-building activities with the same practices, models, and philosophies that have defined what we could call the broadcast era of marketing, where we could pay to have our message communicated over and over again in a controlled environment that was pretty much guaranteed to have a captive audience. But it just doesn't work anymore. Audiences aren't captive. And the reality is that the broadcast era of marketing is firmly in our rearview mirror. (And the only time that driving in the rearview mirror is effective is when you are going backward.)

The media environment that we could describe as the broadcast era has been replaced with what the theoretical physicist Michael Goldhaber coined "the Attention Economy," where goods, and information about them, are abundant and the only thing in scarce supply is attention.

Mr. Goldhaber was interviewed by the *New York Times* in 2021, and he commented on a dynamic he had predicted and written about forty years earlier by saying, "Attention has always been currency, but as we've begun to live our lives increasingly online, it's now the currency. Any discussion of power is now, ultimately, a conversation about attention and how we extract it, wield it, waste it, abuse it, sell it, lose it, and profit from it."

Attention is power.

Attention is not easily bought. But it can be earned. And to earn it, we need to think differently about communication, marketing, branding, and the environment we are operating in. We need to think less about competing for share of market, share of category, or share of wallet, and more about competing for share of culture.

That is the intuitive skill that the successful modern marketers and cultural mavens have brought to bear—a new way of thinking about business and brands that is distinct from the state of mind of the broadcast era. An approach to consumers, and to brands, that is different. Marketing that is conversational, engaging, and shareable. That doesn't rely on controlled messages because it can't. And that relies instead on platforms or ideas that will be amplified, built upon, and often modified by a third party: journalists, influencers, and regular folk.

Make America great again. Yes, we can. Be a local. For the love of sleep.

Often, those ideas and platforms are created and made famous in a repeatable, systematic way, with a clear sense of communication and brand theory to guide their development. But at least equally often, they are not. So, there is a clear opportunity to align the tools, processes, and ambitions of this new marketing with its increasing strategic importance. There is an opportunity to apply the same level of strategic rigor to marketing in the Attention Economy that has been applied to the paid disciplines for the last seventy years of the broadcast-marketing era.

Because that is the surest way to get marketing working again.

PART ONE

A NEW MARKETING PARADIGM

A MODERN MEDIA ISSUE

The most successful brands in all categories have either implicitly or explicitly understood that popularity builds brands and drives market share (we'll dive a little further into the details of that later). And they have created marketing strategies and tactics that have relentlessly built on their popularity year after year after year.

At the heart of most of those strategies—particularly in the US but also, generally speaking, in most developed consumer markets—was paid-media advertising, and in particular the TV campaign.

For most of the last seventy years, advertising, and particularly TV advertising, has been a phenomenally efficient way for smart, creative marketers to make their brands more likable and more popular.

Television was a fabulously effective way of reaching a large audience with a controlled message. And the marketers who focused their TV advertising on creating entertaining interactions with their audience were rewarded with mass-market popularity that drove their market share to levels significantly higher than their competitors'.

On one level, it may seem that the costs associated with creating and running TV commercials are huge. But when you break that cost down into the price you pay to reach one individual with a controlled message, it becomes (or at least became) ridiculously cheap.

Even in the days of multimillion-dollar production budgets, with big-name directors making thirty-second movies, those costs were amortized over many billions of ad impressions. And even though it seems outrageous every year when we hear the latest cost of a Super Bowl commercial, marketers know that they will reach 110 million people with that commercial. (And many more if they focus on using earned media to build that audience pre- and post-game.)

But that effect is eroding. For sixty or seventy years, there was an unwritten contract between media owner (NBC, Fox) and media consumer (you and me) that stated, "I heretofore commit that I shall provide, free of charge, forty-five minutes of entertaining scripted content for every sixty minutes of airtime; with those remaining fifteen minutes being provided to advertisers who will woo you with their appeals." That contract is broken.

The content got worse because it got cheaper—think reality TV. And people began to pay the media owner themselves for the privilege of not watching advertising at all. That, in turn, created a new golden era of TV, where, first, networks like HBO and Showtime began creating their own provocative, entertaining, and highly awarded movies and shows. And then streaming services like Netflix, Hulu, and Amazon flew in and did the same. The quality of the content on ad-free premium services increased dramatically (no pun intended), and people were happy to pay for the quality.

Now, media owners earn three times as much money from consumers as they do from advertisers. And it's no small amount of money. The media industry generates around $200 billion per year, and $150 billion of that is paid to them directly by consumers. $150 billion! Fifteen years ago, regular folks paid almost nothing to media companies, and now they pay them Dr. Evil amounts of money—picture a media executive with a pinky finger raised to the corner of their mouth.

The effect of this was to reduce the size of the audience for advertising-supported TV networks. But the media owners still need to make a profit, so they continued to sell their advertising space for the same amount of money. And what that means is that what used to be a cheap and effective way of communicating to large groups of people has become much more expensive and much less effective.

Here's an example of a media owner charging more for what turned out to be a demonstrably smaller audience (and, to reinforce the point, in this case, the content didn't get worse).

In the run-up to the 2016 Olympics, Steve Burke, CEO of NBCUniversal, prophesied a nightmare scenario. In a press conference, after signing a deal worth $12 billion to host the Olympics until 2032, he said, "[My nightmare is that] we wake up someday and ratings are down 20 percent." Unfortunately for him, that *someday* came all too soon.

Prime-time coverage of Rio 2016 delivered an average nightly audience of 24.5 million live-plus-same-day viewers across seventeen nights—a 21 percent decline from the 2012 London Olympics' prime-time average of 31.1 million.

The network also delivered a 14.5 household rating, which represents a 17 percent decline from 2012's 17.5 and was far below "the high teens."[1] Twenty-one percent audience decline. And a 17 percent ratings decline.

Now, for any marketer who had invested heavily, that was troubling. And there were lots of them. Even with a declining audience, NBC had managed to secure $1.26 billion in advertising spend, which was a full 20 percent higher than for the London Olympics in 2012.

So, 20 percent more advertising dollars were spent on an audience that was 20 percent smaller. That's a bad equation. At the time, Vulture.com (*New York* magazine's pop culture site) commented that:

> Not even the Olympics are immune to audience erosion. Broadcast networks have been dealing with sizable linear ratings declines for more than a decade now prompted by time-shifting technologies … streaming and video on demand.

This trend hasn't slowed down. The audience for the 2022 Beijing Winter Olympics was the smallest ever for a Winter Games—an average of only 11.4 million viewers each night across all platforms, broadcast and streaming (down from an average of 19.8 million viewers for the Pyeongchang Games in 2018). This highlights an issue that has been a decade in the making.

"THE NUMBER OF TRADITIONAL TV VIEWERS IS SHRINKING." As this headline from the *New York Times* beautifully elucidates, nowhere is the shift away from traditional TV viewership more evident than in "Premiere Week."

For those of you outside the US, Premiere Week has been a staple of the television calendar for the last fifty years. It's the week in early fall, right around back-to-school time, when all the big-bet shows from the networks debut. These are the shows that were the focus of the media cattle market that is the "Upfronts," where advertisers buy chunks of airtime from the networks in advance based on the quality of their programming and the audiences they forecast as a result.

In the three years prior to 2019, Premiere Week deliveries had fallen 28 percent; in five years, they had dropped 43 percent.

In the 2020 season, Premiere Week was officially a bust. It was largely ignored by the all-important Adults 18–49 demo. And for the first time, one of the big four broadcast networks failed to average a rating of 1.0 in that demographic. (Fewer than 1 million people in a country of 331 million tuned in to watch.)

> While the marketing money continues to roll right in, those brands investing in primetime programming are reaching an ever-diminishing subset of would-be consumers. (*New York Times*)

So, what's going wrong? Well, it's the internet.

For the longest time, the only way to watch video content at home was to pipe it in through a cable provider, buy a DVD, or watch home movies. And then streaming happened.

It seems funny now to think that Netflix's original business model was selling DVDs and offering rentals by mail. It didn't operate as a streaming service until 2007, and it didn't produce a show until 2013. Before then, we really didn't have a choice in how we watched TV. But as broadband adoption accelerated and download speeds increased, that changed fast. Today, 85 percent of Americans use streaming services.[2] (These are commonly called over-the-top services—OTT—and there are over two hundred OTT providers in the US.)[3]

The content on many of those services is objectively better than what traditional cable TV networks offer. Just look at the number of nominations per network at the 2020 Golden Globes award show: Netflix had 70 percent more nominations than all the traditional TV networks *combined.*

So, what happens when people figure out that they can get better content by streaming than from their cable company? They get rid of cable.

By the end of 2023, more than 40 percent of TV viewers (fifty-four million people or so) had either cut the cord or never had one. And they didn't feel like they were missing out on anything. In fact, they gained. They saved money (a *Consumer Reports* study found that the average cable customer paid $217.42 per month for their service). They weren't forced to pay for channels they didn't watch. And they didn't have to sit through advertising.

In fact, they were happy to pay for the privilege of not watching advertising, which created a massive turnaround for media owners. Again, in a media market worth over a whopping $2 trillion, only 25 percent of that money comes from advertisers now. (As recently as twenty years ago, practically all the money came from advertisers.) The rest comes straight from the pockets of the viewing audience. And they are happy to pay.

Even those folk who still watch cable TV are increasingly recording shows to watch later (time-shifting). Every TV genre (except for children's shows) gets a significant bump in ratings from recorded programs—even, surprisingly, live sports.

The audience for primetime dramas is a full third higher when you add time-shifted viewers. The effect is even bigger for sitcoms, which see a 50 percent lift.[1]

Therein lies the modern media issue: as advertising gets increasingly expensive, the audience for it gets increasingly small.

And it gets worse...

---

[1] Lifts that popular programming genres receive from time-shifting, Nielsen Company 2019.

A MODERN MARKETING PARADOX

Just to rub salt into the wound, let's season that issue with a little pinch of paradox.

The thing is, we may be watching less TV and consuming less traditional media overall (newspapers and magazines haven't performed very well in recent years either). But we're not consuming less media. In fact, we are consuming more—much, much more.

The statistics vary. On the conservative side, it's reported that the average American consumes thirteen hours of media every day. We either watch, read, search, play, listen, or otherwise engage with some form of media.

Less conservative reporting has us enveloped by a whopping eighteen hours of media every day. Now, the astute mathematicians among you will have quickly figured out that this leaves only six hours for everything else—you know, cooking, eating, sleeping, walking the dog, brushing your teeth. And six hours is not a lot of time. So, there may be some very unhappy, or at least slightly overweight, dogs in America right now.

It sounds almost impossible that we engage with media so much—that is, until you think about how many social media accounts you have. On average, we have 8.7. Sounds like a lot, but just count your own. You may quickly realize that you are one of the people pushing the average up rather than down.

And, of course, where would our social media consumption be without the smartphone? In 2010, only 20 percent of us owned a smartphone. In 2024, 86 percent of us worldwide did. In fact, it's almost hard to believe that there are still 14 percent of people living through the ignominy of not having one—until you think about very young kids who can't use them and very old people who still don't know how to open a PDF.

Elon Musk now talks about the population of developed countries as *symbionts*. In nature, that's one organism living in symbiosis with another. Like the feeder fish that live in symbiosis with sharks, eating their dead skin and parasites—providing a service (cleaning) and extracting a fee (food) simultaneously. In Musk-land, the symbiont is us, living in symbiosis with our smartphones. And let's face it: they are almost permanently attached to our hands. In fact, those pesky hands are the one thing that's getting in the way of us unleashing the full power of the supercomputer we carry around all day. We simply can't type fast enough. Our fingers are a very inefficient interface, which is why Elon is developing technologies that can connect our brains directly to our phones. Imagine how much media we'll consume then!

So, we're consuming more and more media, and increasingly, we're consuming that media in digital formats. Podcasts, digital radio, streaming movies, Twitter feeds, Facebook groups, Instagram Stories, TikTok, YouTube influencers, Twitch streams. And you have to imagine that when we go full symbiont, we'll consume all our media in digital formats—who wants to read a physical newspaper when your brain is wired to your phone?

And the simple truth is this: when we consume media in digital formats, the last thing most of us want is for it to be disrupted by advertising. It's why so many of us are paying so much money directly to media owners for premium, ad-free services. But even if we're a little cheap and we take the free, ad-supported version, it's very easy to skip the ads. And skip them we do.

On average, 47 percent of us skip ads. That might not be surprising. What might be, though, is when you ask the same question of the members of Generation Z, that number jumps to a massive 82 percent! That is a glimpse of a very near future.

So, a paradox on top of the issue. As advertising gets more expensive, the audience for that advertising becomes smaller. And as we consume more media, we watch less advertising.

A COMPOUND PROBLEM

Surely to goodness it can't get any worse! Well, I'm afraid it can. In media terms, marketers are facing a triple threat: higher costs for smaller audiences; people consuming more media and watching less advertising; and, finally, marketers now must divert significant chunks of their budgets into areas that didn't used to exist (or that were paid for by other parts of the organization), so, in relative terms, their budgets are getting smaller.

I'm sure most everyone is familiar with the concept of the marketing funnel, where large groups of people become aware of the brand at the mouth of the funnel, but as those folks get closer to considering purchase of the brand and, ultimately, actually buying it, the size of the group gets progressively smaller. Let's use that to illustrate the issue.

In days of yore (you know, in 2005 or so), people who made their way to the bottom of the funnel generally ended up at some kind of physical retail outlet. They were in a supermarket figuring out which toothpaste to buy, or a car dealership kicking tires, or a Nordstrom trying on dresses. In every instance, the brand owner—Colgate or Nissan or Anne Klein—was paying some kind of fee or incentive to the retailer to push their product.

These could range from stocking fees in supermarkets to sales incentives or co-op advertising funds to local car dealers. Fees like that were a significant part of what made the bottom of the funnel work—the little nudge that could sway the decision at the point of purchase in favor of your brand. The job of paying those fees and incentives generally lay with the organization's sales team, who did not report into the corporate marketing team but sat alongside them. (This is different in some categories and in some markets where the sales team is part of the marketing organization, but in large US companies, this is a common structure.) The important point here is that the budget for those sales incentives sat with the sales team.

Fast-forward twenty years. Increasingly now, the bottom of the funnel does not happen at a physical location but online. We're buying toothpaste on Amazon, shopping for cars on Carvana, and ordering outfits from Rent the Runway. The difference is that the responsibility for online sales almost always falls within the marketing department. And because of the increased availability and accuracy of online sales data, that job has been given increased visibility and is under daily scrutiny.

In turn, the digital tools available to marketers have become ever more sophisticated. SEO and SEM are massive media industries. Amazon generated almost $46 billion in advertising revenue in 2023 from manufacturers who wanted to juice their product sales. And Amazon is a relative newbie to generating ad revenues! Google, which has been at it longer, earned almost $238 billion in ad revenues. Programmatic digital-display advertising, shopping cart optimization, customer data management—they are all huge costs for marketers. But in real terms, they play the same role as physical retailers did in the days before e-commerce. Google and Amazon advertising are essentially doing the same things for your brand that a supermarket stocking fee did: giving you visibility at the sharp point of the point of sale. It's not creating broad awareness; it's not building any deeper affinity for your brand; it's simply making you available to buy to an audience already showing signs of interest in buying from you. But the unfortunate reality is that without diverting huge amounts of advertising funds to the oligarchy of Amazon and Google, without paying them their tax simply to have your product be found, your tube of toothpaste will be left dusty and lonely in the corner of a digital shelf.

There's no denying the need to focus on these activities. There's also no hiding from the fact that what gets measured gets done. And it's very easy to measure, in great detail, digital-marketing performance metrics.

But it raises an important issue: costs at the bottom of the funnel are big and getting bigger every year. That's $284 billion in payments to Google and Amazon alone. Add in Meta, and the total rises to over $400 billion. These payments used to be covered by the sales team. Now they are paid by the marketing department. And marketing department budgets haven't gotten bigger, so they've taken the money from somewhere else: the top of the funnel, where the brand is built.

And, as surely as yin needs yang, the bottom of the funnel only works if people keep arriving at the top of the funnel. Sadly, however, that appears not to be happening.

Les Binet and Peter Field are marketing scientists largely revered in the world of marketing effectiveness for their consistently good and provocative work on providing empirical evidence for what works and why. And they have offered some troubling perspectives on the trend lines for marketing effectiveness.

Short-termism has been increasing, and in lockstep, campaign effectiveness has fallen off a cliff. Spoiler alert: it's getting worse.

The year 2012 appears to be the beginning of the effectiveness decline, which was arguably also the year that social media truly mainstreamed in the US. The marketing for brands that had invested in long-term campaigns fared slightly better than the average, managing to maintain effectiveness until around 2014. But then, they, too, dropped precipitously in effectiveness.

On every measure of effectiveness, the trendline is going south. And a couple of pieces of evidence are offered for why. One is that budgets are going down. The other is that short-termism in the execution of campaigns is rising (where the pressure of quarterly earnings reports is creating a need to boost short-term sales regardless of the impact it has in the long term). I don't disagree with either of the findings. But the situation is unlikely to change.

The reality is that if a marketer has a shopping cart on their website that isn't working properly, they need to fix it. If they don't, then regardless of how brilliant their brand-building activities are, they will be for naught. If people want to buy something from you and they can't buy it because of a technical glitch, they'll go somewhere else real fast.

But the marketer needs to pay for someone to fix that bug. So, it comes out of a marketing budget that previously may have been reserved for longer-term activities. Ten or fifteen years ago, most marketers didn't need to worry about that. Now they worry about it all the time. They didn't used to have to worry about spending millions of dollars on protecting their Google search ranking either. Now they worry about it all the time. Or paying Amazon for preferred placement...and on and on and on. And not to rub too much salt in the wound, but as we focus more attention on optimizing our AI search rankings in addition to our web search rankings, we will be adding another tax bill to the pile.

The industry term for this collective activity is "optimizing the bottom of the funnel." And regardless of how pedestrian it might sound to spend time optimizing the bottom of the funnel when you could be having fun optimizing the top of it, it's unlikely to change any time soon.

To address the decline in effectiveness, Binet and Field suggest that marketers should reprioritize their expenditure in favor of top-of-the-funnel, long-term brand-building activities. But that just doesn't seem practical or achievable. Because the reality for most marketers is that if they don't pay their taxes to Google and Amazon, they simply won't have a business. And right now, that is resulting in the simple fact that close to 70 percent of all advertising spend is on digital media, with Google, Amazon, and Meta raking in the overwhelming share of that money. So, the actual split in marketing spend is closer to 40/60 than 60/40. And unless discretionary long-term marketing budgets increase dramatically to keep pace with the need to divert so much money to the bottom of the funnel, it's just not going to change.

And the perfect storm makes landfall. We're paying more money for smaller audiences, we're consuming more media but seeing less advertising, and marketing budgets are being diverted to the bottom of the funnel, leaving brand building at the top unsupported and underdone.

It may be the end of an era.

THE RISE OF THE ATTENTION ECONOMY

At the end of the 2016 documentary *Supersonic*, about the creation and musical domination of the band Oasis, Noel Gallagher reflected on their pinnacle achievement—playing to 250,000 people over two nights at the Knebworth Rock Festival in 1996. In it, he lamented what he saw as the end of a musical era that, in many ways, reflects the end of a cultural and marketing era.

> It did feel like the end of something rather than the beginning of something. I had a sense that it was never going to happen again. It was the pre-digital age, it was the pre-talent show, reality-TV age. We were about to enter into celebrity-driven culture, and I've always thought that it was the last great gathering of the people before the birth of the internet. (Noel Gallagher, *Supersonic*)

And yet, while he was mourning the end of one era, it was clear that his band's approach to creating their fame and building their b(r)and was an approach that would come to define the era that replaced it.

Central to their approach was their maniacal need for attention—and a well-honed skill for getting it.

> It doesn't matter what they write about us in the press. As long as we're on the cover. They can write anything they want about us inside but as long as we're on the cover, then it don't matter. (Noel Gallagher, *Supersonic*)

Writing about them was something the press did unceasingly. And the band gave them plenty to write about. The first headline-grabbing bonanza came after they were deported from Holland following a riotous ferry crossing that saw Liam Gallagher fighting running battles with West Ham United fans on the ship. And it kept going. The well-publicized sibling rivalry between the brothers. Their view that drug taking was as normal as drinking tea in the UK. They were like catnip to purring British journalists. And, perhaps without realizing it, they were the vanguard of a shift they denounced. They characterized the beginnings of what they referred to as internet-driven celebrity culture, but what economists, academics, and psychologists were already calling the Attention Economy.

In the Attention Economy, we are bombarded by creators, influencers, bloggers, vloggers, TikTok dancers, reality TV celebrities, journalists, TV anchors, politicians, family, and friends who are vying for a little piece of our attention. This makes it tempting to think that this is a very modern dynamic—the inevitable result of our obsession with social media. But the dynamics of the Attention Economy were recognized and written about as far back as the 1960s.

In 1967, the charismatic leader of a group called the Situationist International wrote a manifesto called *The Society of the Spectacle*.[4] In it, he suggested that we were living in a time when "all that was once directly lived has become mere representation." The author's name was Guy Debord, and he was living and writing during the time of the student rebellion and cultural revolution in Paris in 1968.

Debord was critiquing modern capitalism with a central theme: that the philosophy and ideology that had previously framed political and commercial activity had been replaced by performance and spectacle. The ideological reasons for political action were less important than the flourish with which those actions were performed—which, when you think about the actions of Marjorie Taylor Greene, Matt Gaetz, or Alexandria Ocasio-Cortez, may not seem so very far from the reality we are living in today.

The specific idea of "attention economics" was first posited in 1971 by the Nobel Laureate Herbert A. Simon. He introduced the idea that attention was the "bottleneck of human thought" and that "a wealth of information creates a poverty of attention."

In the 1970s through to the early 1990s, this was an interesting thought but arguably not a culturally important one. But in the mid-1990s, as the internet began to achieve mainstream adoption and access to information was democratized, the implications of the idea came into sharp relief.

In 1996 (interestingly, the same year that Oasis played Knebworth), a book called *Rules of the Net* suggested that attention—not information—was "the hard currency of cyberspace." That view was reinforced in a prescient article in *WIRED* magazine in 1997 by the theoretical physicist Michael Goldhaber. He rejected the idea that information was scarce and suggested instead that the commodity in scarce supply was attention. His thesis was that the international economy was shifting from a material-based economy to an attention-based economy, and the phrase "Attention Economy" was born.

Goldhaber himself had been thinking about the implications of the Attention Economy since 1984, consistently referencing the earlier work from Simon:

> What information consumes is rather obvious: it consumes the attention of its recipients. Hence a wealth of information creates a poverty of attention and a need to allocate that attention efficiently among the overabundance of information sources that might consume it.[5]

But Goldhaber's *WIRED* article struck a nerve among an audience of technology fans, and the phrase stuck. But although the Attention Economy has been written about in numerous books and referenced in numerous PhD dissertations since, its implications probably weren't as clear as they have become since the mainstreaming of social media.

What is clear now is the way brands, politicians, and cultural figures are competing for share of the Attention Economy: the approaches they use and the results they generate. And what's interesting is that there are very clear patterns emerging. The patterns suggest an approach to marketing that's quite different from the one that had been successfully employed over the seventy years of the broadcast era. And, in fact, these new approaches often contradict the maxims of broadcast-era marketing.

Arguably, the implications of Attention Economy marketing were seen most clearly in the first presidential campaign (and subsequent reign) of Donald Trump. This is perhaps what prompted Charlie Warzel, an opinion writer for the *New York Times* who studies online extremism, to revisit Goldhaber—the man and his thinking—in 2021 to better understand the media environment that was crashing into view during the early days of the COVID-19 lockdown. He began his piece by writing:

> Here's a short list of things he saw coming: the complete dominance of the internet, increased shamelessness in politics, terrorists co-opting social media, the rise of reality television, personal websites, oversharing, personal essay, fandoms and online influencer culture—along with the near destruction of our ability to focus.

And in predicting those things, he recognized, as Warzel writes, that:

> Attention has always been currency, but as we've begun to live our lives increasingly online, it's now <u>the</u> currency. Any discussion of power is now, ultimately, a conversation about attention and how we extract it, wield it, waste it, abuse it, sell it, lose it and profit from it.[6]

People who can command the most attention become the most powerful. Perhaps that's always been true. But when the command of attention is democratized—as it has been with social media—the importance of the Attention Economy is magnified.

And there is no question that the command of attention has been democratized.

Anyone with a phone can broadcast to an international audience in the tens of millions. You don't need to be Donald J. Trump to get billions of likes. Khaby Lame is a Senegalese teenager living in suburban Italy who amassed nearly 123 million followers and two billion likes on TikTok. Keith Gill (DeepFuckingValue) is the value investor with a massive Reddit following who upended the global investing market with the meme-stock rally of GameStop. Nathan Tankus was a twenty-eight-year-old undergraduate at John Jay College in New York whose writing on monetary policy was being followed by members of the Federal Reserve.

The people, movements, and brands that understand the dynamics of the Attention Economy are the ones that prosper within it. Obama and Trump. Uber and Tesla. Oasis and Nathan Tankus. All of them, whether consciously or not, recognize what Goldhaber reminded Charlie Warzel at the end of their interview.

"The fundamental thing is that you can't escape the Attention Economy."

PART TWO

LEARNING FROM MODERN MARKETERS

"Only a crisis—actual or perceived—
produces real change. When that crisis
occurs, the actions that are taken depend
on the ideas that are lying around."

(MILTON FRIEDMAN)

BUILDING NEW BRANDS
IN NEW WAYS

Middletown, Connecticut, is a fairly anonymous, post-industrial town that sits, unsurprisingly, in the middle of the state of Connecticut. It is a quiet town of around forty thousand people on the west bank of the Connecticut River, with few things to distinguish it other than a surprisingly wide variety of international cuisines and the campus of Wesleyan University.

But, slightly paradoxically, Middletown is also the birthplace of the grandly named Institute for the Future. The institute was founded in 1968 and operates to this day—although now in the more future-facing town of Palo Alto.

In 1970, the institute was taken over by a systems engineer named Roy Amara. Under his direction, the group conducted some of the earliest studies of ARPANET, the structural precursor to the modern internet. But perhaps Amara's most enduring contribution to our cultural conversation is what has become known as Amara's Law.

The law is simple. It states:

> We tend to overestimate the effect of a tech-
> nology in the short run and underestimate the
> effect in the long run.

Amara was particularly sensible in not putting hard time-
lines on his law. His short and long runs are not governed by
months or years. And as a result, the law has held true over a
long period of time. For example, the mainframe digital computer was developed to some fanfare at the end of World War
II, and one can imagine that in those early days, the immediate
transformative power of computing was overplayed. But then in
1977 (over thirty years later), the head of the Digital Equipment
Corporation, one of the most powerful computing companies
in the world at the time and, next to IBM, the largest manufacturer of mainframe computers, significantly underestimated
the long-term role of computing and personal computers when
he declared, "There is no reason that anyone would want a
computer in their home." (Now, of course, we carry computers
more powerful than DEC's multimillion-dollar mainframes in
our pockets.) As Amara predicted, we overestimated the effect
of the computer in the short run, and we underestimated it in
the long run.

This example illustrates another pattern that is often seen
in the technology adoption cycle: there is initial hype, which is
answered by "rational" cynicism before the promise of a technology is ultimately realized. This pattern was illustrated and popularized by the Gartner Group, which branded it the hype cycle.

The dot-com boom offers a good example of it in practice.
It started around 1995 with the massive and exuberant adoption

of new internet platforms, which was answered by the rational cynicism of the Nobel Prize–winning economist Paul Krugman, who predicted that "by 2005 or so, it will become clear that the internet's impact on the economy has been no greater than the fax machine's." And now, of course, there isn't an aspect of our lives that isn't touched in one or many ways by the internet, and its impact is only strengthening. Hype, cynicism, realization.

A perfect example of the hype cycle has played out in the world of marketing and marketing communications over the last fifteen or twenty years.

It started in 2005, after the dust had settled on the dot-com boom and its subsequent bust, when the first shoots in the spring of social media were beginning to flower.

In April that year, Bob Garfield, the editor at large for advertising industry publication *Ad Age*, wrote a widely circulated and widely discussed article titled "The Chaos Scenario."[7]

The central theme was that the mass-marketing era (which had been created by the ability of paid advertising to reach millions of people with controlled marketing messages) was over—and that a new era of consumer control and participation was upon us. He wrote:

> Advertising. Branding. Distribution. Consumer research. Product development. Manufacturing. They will all be turned upside down as the despotism of the executive suite gives way to the will, and wisdom, of the masses in a new commercial and cultural epoch.

He wasn't the only one ploughing this furrow. That same year, *Time* magazine picked "YOU" (us) as their Person (people) of the Year, recognizing the millions of people contributing to the cultural discourse by generating user content on Facebook, YouTube... (and even Myspace).

Garfield's future was embraced and adopted with enthusiasm. A slew of new advertising and communications agencies opened to help clients take advantage of it. (One of them launched their business with a symbolic burial service to recognize the death of the thirty-second commercial.) New media companies opened their virtual doors and grew quickly with reporting that was provocative and unchecked. Garfield himself went on to turn his "Chaos Scenario" article into a *Chaos Scenario* book in 2009.

But (as Roy Amara might have predicted) the initial hype was answered with an inevitable cynicism—a view that mass marketing and the mass-media advertising that supported it were an inviolable part of building businesses in market economies.

Many of the cynical voices came from traditional media companies, which was perhaps not unexpected. As Upton Sinclair once noted, "It's difficult to get a man to understand something when their salary depends on them not understanding it." And the salaries of traditional media companies (and the ecosystem they supported) were entirely dependent upon them reinforcing the notion that mass marketing through traditional media channels was alive and well.

But the most damning cynicism in this instance came in the form of a clever, though cynical, business move perpetrated by what was then Facebook (now Meta).

In the early days of Facebook, many new media companies, publishers, and business owners spent their time building a fan base on the platform, a place where they could share their own news and content and, in turn, create more fans and more passion around their brand. "Liking" brands and publishers was part of the social media experience. And seeing the content from the brands and publishers you liked was widely enjoyed.

But in 2011, Facebook changed its algorithm. The first change was to the news feed, which it took control of. Instead of the feed being populated with the latest news from your base of Facebook friends, it would now be populated by "Top" news. And the definition of "Top" was within Facebook's control.

The way it exercised that control was to reduce the organic exposure of content that came from brands and publishers. The message was simple: if you want to reach an audience on Facebook, you must pay Facebook to reach that audience—even if you've spent time and money building your own audience on the "social" platform.

The algorithm changed again in 2013 to tighten the screws. This time, the effect was particularly damaging for the new-media publishers that had come to rely on their Facebook audience seeing content they published.

In a *New York Times* article in 2017, Nicole Ames, who ran a digital marketing firm called Twist IMC, commented that "you spent years building up this organic following, and now your content no longer shows up unless you pay."

The algorithm change was accompanied by a full-court press on the part of the massive media sales team at Facebook, who paraded through marketing organizations and media companies to announce that organic reach was dead—that Facebook was "pay to play."

And indeed, it was. According to *Forbes* magazine, by 2015, organic reach on Facebook averaged 2 percent. So, for every one thousand fans a brand or publisher had on the platform, only twenty would see the content they posted.

On the one hand, Facebook argued that this benefited the user. They were more likely to see content from their friends when organic content from third parties was deprioritized. But, of course, it benefited Facebook more by freeing up more news feed space to be sold to brands at the ultimate expense of content from your friends.

And Upton Sinclair's comment began to seem even more prescient. The people whose salaries depended on them reinforcing the importance of paid media were happy to "pay to play."

Inevitably, Facebook's actions dampened the flames of Garfield's Chaos Scenario, and many marketers eased back into a cadence of business as usual.

Hype led to cynicism, which, for many marketers, led to apathy.

But for others, the hype led to action.

Although it would be accurate to say that (contrary to Garfield's prediction) chaos didn't ensue in 2006, it would be equally accurate to observe that, in the years that followed, opportunity did arise for brands and people who understood, and tried to shape, as Garfield himself put it, "the will, and wisdom, of the masses."

#WOKEUPLIKETHIS—
THE CREATION
OF GLOSSIER

Emily Weiss was studying at NYU when she started a three-day-a-week internship at *Teen Vogue*—a position that scored her an appearance on the reality TV show *The Hills*. She graduated in 2007, spent some time working for *W* magazine, then moved to grown-up *Vogue* as a fashion assistant. In that role, hanging out at shoots with famous models, stylists, and makeup artists, she developed the idea for a real-world, behind-the-scenes look at the beauty routines of the famous and the fabulous. The insider tips. The products they really loved. From Japanese skin cream to Blistex lip balm. She started a blog and called it *Into the Gloss*.

The blog grew in popularity quickly. The candid beauty-regimen interviews she conducted with the celebrities she was assisting were collected in a section called "Top Shelf," and they developed a cult following. Regular beauty enthusiasts started participating in the online conversation, adding their own thoughts and recommendations to topics that were published.

In 2010, she quit the Condé Nast organization and started running *Into the Gloss* full-time with editorial director Nick Axelrod, who came from the publishing world.

The blog was enjoying success as a stand-alone publishing operation, but Weiss quickly realized that there was gold in the mine of information she was collecting from her readers on their opinions of the beauty industry and its products.

What became clear was that there was a disconnect between the tens of thousands of people actively contributing to the beauty conversation on the blog and the massive beauty industry that served them. The industry's approach to the beauty conversation was top-down: "We'll tell you what's best for you." Science would lead to product innovation, which would lead to the commercialization of the product, which would lead to an advertising campaign to tell women how to become more beautiful.

What Weiss saw in her work at *Vogue* and in the conversations online was that there were no absolutes in beauty. Everyone was different, and everyone's beauty regimen was different. As a result, people didn't like dictates on beauty. They liked conversations about beauty.

> I got a master's in the state of beauty through Into the Gloss, all the weird hang-ups people have about beauty, and the double standards. How beauty can break down walls, and how beauty is something that every single person everywhere in the world deals with. It's really foundational to who you are and how you relate.[8]

She also noticed that the majority of items in the beauty arsenal of celebrities were skincare products—not makeup. That the foundation of beauty—having skin that looked as good as it could—was more important than the decoration.

> One of the things I realized really early was that at every makeup artist's table, they'd lay out all their products from their kit, and almost half of the stuff was skincare... In order for your makeup to look better, start with a skincare routine.[9]

Those two simple insights birthed the idea of Glossier, a democratic, people-powered beauty brand that focuses on skincare products.

SKIN FIRST, MAKEUP SECOND, SMILE ALWAYS.

In Weiss's mind, brand was everything. She wanted to create a beauty brand that people would wear on a sweatshirt. A brand that was about more than the products—or the product category—but about helping to give people a voice and to unlock their innate power. (As opposed to "empowering women," which she felt was a patronizing concept.)

Importantly, the brand had to be about more than the personality of its founder (indeed, she celebrated her anonymity when she toured new store openings). In her view, the brand had to be grounded in a truth about its reason for being, its origin story, the why behind its existence.

The Glossier brand's philosophy is captured in the line: *Skin First, Makeup Second, Smile Always*—a truth consistent with the defining insight behind the business: that great beauty regimens start with skincare first. (The foundation before the decoration.)

The brand's aesthetic was anchored in the use of "millennial pink" and a photographic style that was representative of the slightly rose-tinted reality that came to define the Instagram generation. Glossier's models were consistent in their inconsistency.

They were often crowdsourced from among the brand's millions of social media followers and diverse in every way: ethnically, culturally, and physically. Facial features that may have been considered blemishes in broadcast beauty culture—freckles, acne scars, bushy eyebrows—were celebrated as symbols of individuality and inclusive beauty.

At retail, the brand came to life in stores that were almost theatrical. Pink-hued and scented with Glossier perfume, the stores were physical manifestations of the brand, complete with a multitude of Instagram-ready corners, six-foot-tall tubes of Boy Brow (one of their signature products), and millennial-pink-jumpsuit-clad "editors" to help you document your visit. The Glossier store was not retail designed to sell; it was retail designed to experience the brand. If you wanted to simply buy something, it was much easier to order online and pick it up.

The Glossier brand, its brand truth, and its aesthetic have been adhered to in a way that traditional marketers might have described as slavish. And yet, there's nothing about it that feels like hard work. In fact, it feels effortless. When you scan through the Glossier Instagram feed, for example, it is difficult to separate the brand-produced content from the user-generated content. All of it delivers the same feeling.

And that is the real power of the brand. Because while the branding of Glossier was important, arguably, it was the participatory nature of the brand building that was central to its success.

Participation was embedded into the Glossier operating model from inception. Indeed, it was the fan conversation on *Into the Gloss* that sparked the idea for the brand. But conversation wasn't treated as a promotional technique; it was actively embraced as part of the product development and innovation process.

The motivation for participation was as commercially smart as it was altruistic.

> "Sixty percent of Americans rely on peer-to-peer recommendations on whether they decide to buy a beauty product. It could be someone on social media they've never met before, or it could be someone they read about on *Into the Gloss*," she said. "People are the 'unlock' to shopping today [because] whatever you consider buying, you've probably read a review about it."

Which leads Weiss to exhort other businesspeople to: *Find ways to ask your customers questions and build that into what you do.*

But participation doesn't happen in a vacuum. (Without action, there is no reaction.) And in this instance, the action came in the form of a tirelessly executed content-marketing program.

Henry Davis is the president and CFO of the brand, and in an article with Forbes, he stated that: *The best thing we can do is give people content...That is our main driver of growth.*

The Glossier feed is a well-curated collection of product and lifestyle content. Simple product posts—single-product photography and product collections—sit alongside beauty how-to videos. User-generated content is featured heavily, including imagery and retweeted posts. Occasional brand content is featured—sale announcements, for example. Skincare routines are filmed and posted, both by the brand and by its followers. Other whimsical offshoots of the main Glossier channels also developed: @dogsofglossier and @glossierboyfriends both attracted tens of thousands of followers on Instagram.

And, of course, the combination of Glossier's website and channels with the *Into the Gloss* blog created a closed-loop ecosystem, where each content engine supported the other and drove traffic back and forth. (On Instagram, for example, Glossier has over three million followers, which combines with one million followers of *Into the Gloss*.)

It all worked. Glossier launched in 2014. And by staying steadfastly true to the brand, making it easy for fans to participate in the brand's world—even down to defining which products would be developed—and creating a palpable sense of energy through compelling, beautifully produced content marketing, the company had surpassed $100 million in revenue by early 2020 and achieved unicorn status with a valuation of $1.2 billion.

Ten years after *Into the Gloss* and six years after the brand was launched, Glossier stumbled. At the peak of cancel culture— toward the end of 2020—a group of former employees accused Glossier of fostering a hostile workplace that stood in contrast to its brand of inclusivity. After some initial stumbles in its response, the company made strategic and operational changes that aggressively realigned it with its core truth and operating principles. Emily Weiss transitioned from CEO to executive chairwoman, the company made renewed commitments to community building and operational transparency, and it changed working requirements to make the company more accessible to BIPOC employees. That return to its core truth reinvigorated the brand, and the gloss returned. And it was accelerated by a renewed commitment to their original communications platform, *Into the Gloss*, and a new focus on influencer partnerships to drive conversation and talkability.

By 2023, the company had inked a distribution deal with Sephora and seen a sales increase of 73 percent, marking its biggest year ever. And, even in the face of new celebrity-backed beauty brands, Glossier endured, with market-leading awareness and "intent to repurchase" rates being recorded.

So, even after a public stumble, a clear and recommitted focus on the foundational truth of the brand and a reenergized approach to creating cultural conversation brought the smile back to Glossier.

A NEW KIND OF CAR—
THE DOMINANCE
OF TESLA

Like Glossier, as of writing in mid-2025, Tesla has hit a couple of speed bumps. The famously mercurial founder, Elon Musk, has disenfranchised a portion of the Tesla customer base with words and actions that felt out of kilter with the Tesla brand. As a result, sales in key markets—and particularly sales of certain models like the Cybertruck—have taken a significant hit, and market capitalization plunged in the first quarter of this year. However, a consistent aspect of the Attention Economy is that people are fickle, memories are short, and brands remain resilient.

In 2013, Tesla's share of the global automotive market was too small to measure—a rounding error. By 2018, the company had captured 1.4 percent of the market by revenue, from a standing start in just five years. That number put them just outside the top ten of all automotive manufacturers. It was an increase of 250 percent between 2017 and 2018. By the end of 2024, Tesla had amassed around 12 percent of the global car market. Perhaps even more impressively, in 2024, Tesla's market capitalization had surpassed $1 trillion—making up almost half the market capitalization of the entire automotive industry and equal to the capitalization of the next twenty-five or so automotive companies combined.

Now, those numbers are impressive. But let's not forget the obvious: Tesla only makes electric cars. In 2024, electric cars only accounted for 16 percent of the global automotive market. They're not even on the playing field for 84 percent of the game, and yet they are still winning.

As noted, both sales and market capitalization dipped in 2025. But context and timeline are important. For example, although market capitalization appeared to fall off a cliff, it fell from an inflated high (so, more like falling out of a hot air balloon than off a cliff). In May 2025, Tesla shares are trading for around $300, up from around $175 in May 2024. And although sales are dipping, they are dipping most in Northern Europe and California—arguably, the markets where Musk's recent stance seemed most at odds with a brand at the center of a promised sustainable future.

And that disconnect may prove to be the undoing of the Tesla brand. But I'm not confident that it will. The Tesla business is unquestionably connected to sustainable energy. But the truth of the Tesla brand sits outside that category definition.

Tesla and SpaceX are both brands defined by the worldview and values of the founder. And Musk's worldview is about solving great problems and pursuing great dreams. His approach to problem-solving is rule-breaking and swashbuckling, almost piratical or anarchic. And he has dreamt the biggest dreams. He is on record as trying to solve problems in areas that will truly affect humanity. And the three he has focused on are the internet, space travel, and sustainable energy. Interestingly, the problem he set out to solve with Tesla wasn't that carbon emissions were destroying the planet (although I'm sure that factored in) but that fossil fuels would run out, and we needed a sustainable alternative before they did.

His focused and consistent approach to feverish innovation has been impressive. It built the Tesla brand into something that was admired for both its future-facing worldview and its elegant, almost fetishistic, engineering and aesthetic. And it has resulted in what is, objectively, a powerful brand.

There are several consultancies that measure the value of brands using various methodologies, and Tesla has found a place in their rankings. In 2020, Tesla was ranked as the ninety-fifth most valuable US brand in research company Kantar's list of the top one hundred. In 2019, the company took forty-fifth place in brand consultancy Prophet's Brand Relevance Index. By 2023, they were ranked as the twelfth most powerful brand by Interbrand.

And what is most interesting is how that brand was created, which, consistent with Tesla's approach to design, manufacturing, and sales, broke all the rules of traditional broadcast-era marketing.

Tesla previewed its first-ever car, the Roadster, to an invited group of 350 people in July 2006. In November that year, it appeared at the San Francisco Auto Show. In December, it was featured in *Time* magazine as the best invention of 2006.

The first one hundred Roadsters sold out in three weeks.

From that day to this, Tesla has spent zero dollars on broadcast advertising. They don't spend any advertising money on the major social platforms either—Facebook, Instagram, TikTok, or YouTube. Every other automotive manufacturer does. Many of them spend a great deal of money with those digital media owners. And yet, Tesla tops them all in terms of organic engagement on those platforms.

That isn't an accident. Tesla is consistently earning attention for its brand and its products. Elon Musk is an impressive medium himself. Clearly, as the owner of the platform, he has a substantial following on X/Twitter. Interestingly, though, while he had an impressive seventy-something million followers on the platform before he bought it in 2022, he now has over 220 million followers, and that number keeps on increasing.

He also makes himself widely available to the media—both traditional and modern. Sometimes that level of visibility can backfire, as it appears to have done in the first quarter of 2025. But very often, his physical or virtual presence is a boon to his brands and businesses. More than that, though, the actions of Tesla consistently generate earned media attention and reinforce brand perceptions of provocative innovation.

Those actions are varied. Not the classic combination of product announcement, press release, and interview circuit that defined the traditional world of earned media. Instead, every aspect of the company's actions, from their product design to their retail approaches to their publicity-driving activities, drives engagement and conversation.

They make their product launches truly noteworthy. SpaceX—Musk's private NASA—launched the Falcon Heavy, the world's most powerful rocket, by attaching one of Tesla's Roadsters to it (complete with a mannequin dressed as an astronaut). And it generated massive amounts of online and offline conversation about both the Tesla and the SpaceX brands as a result.

They focus on truly noteworthy design. The Cybertruck—whether you like it or not—was a game-changing piece of automotive design. Not only was its exoskeleton made from the same material as the SpaceX Starship shell, but its design was also purposefully evocative of both the vehicle in *Blade Runner* and James Bond's Lotus Esprit in *The Spy Who Loved Me*. And that combination of Gen X schoolboy dreams made waves both inside and outside the industry. (Even the fact that, during the press launch, they managed to break the unbreakable windows was celebrated and amplified—once again, even negative press can amplify a message.)

They also look for opportunities to engage in social purpose that supports their brand, like famously releasing all their patents in an effort to save the earth.

Every one of Tesla's actions communicates something about the brand, from their design aesthetic to their launch stunts to the proclamations of their founder. The stronger the connection to the foundational truth of the Tesla brand, and the more authentic the action used to communicate that truth, the more powerfully it establishes the brand. And, of course, vice versa—which makes Tesla such an interesting case study to examine.

Tesla has built its brand by consistently earning attention—being in the news and being part of the cultural conversation for doing things that are provocative, talkable, and headline-grabbing. And for twenty years, those actions were consistent with the core truth of the Tesla brand: its piratical innovation and big dreaming. And as a result, the Tesla brand reflected well on the people who bought it or liked to talk about it because they considered themselves to be innovators and dreamers.

But when those headline-grabbing actions were inconsistent with the Tesla brand, they reflected poorly on the people who bought Tesla or liked to talk about it. And the brand and the business suffered as a result.

What's interesting is that the words—and particularly the actions—of Elon Musk that have most affected Tesla recently are not so very far away from the words and actions that made Tesla great in the first place. Both SpaceX and Tesla were made viable as businesses through a relentless focus on cost-cutting and process improvement. It became a hallmark of Musk's leadership style. And when that modus operandi was connected to big dreams like a sustainable future and space travel, it was dramatic, entrepreneurial, and exciting. But when cost-cutting and process improvement were disconnected from big dreams—like making Twitter/X more profitable or using DOGE to make the US government more cost-efficient—it was mean-spirited and unempathetic.

A clear communication of the philosophical truth of the Tesla brand, presented in ways that were provocative, talkable, and attention-grabbing, built a powerful Tesla brand.

But when the philosophical truth was lost to an operational truth, those same provocative and attention-grabbing actions (like using a chainsaw to announce cuts to the federal budget) damaged the brand.

Which leads to an inevitable conclusion for Tesla: if it can focus on its foundational truth of solving big problems and dreaming big dreams—and communicate that truth in its provocative and headline-grabbing ways—then the brand will be back on smooth roads.

YES, WE CAN— OBAMA 2008

There's a law in thermodynamics called the law of conservation of energy, which basically says that in an enclosed system, energy can't be destroyed; it can only be transferred. So, for example, the energy that is expended in rubbing two sticks together isn't lost; it is simply transferred into heat—a different kind of energy— and the amount of heat is proportional to the amount of effort that is put into rubbing the sticks together.

All social networks (communities or groups) are enclosed systems, and all of them generate their own energy. Some of them are small and placid. Some of them are big, vocal, and highly energetic. Some of them start out small and placid, only to become big, vocal, and highly energetic. Increasingly, the most successful brands are those that best harness the energy of these digital societies—and any brand, in any category, has the ability to do it.

Importantly, it's not just consumer brands that understand this dynamic. Many of the most impactful cultural phenomena in the last fifteen years have also executed the same plays from the same playbook. In fact, you could argue that modern politicians and their progressive campaign infrastructures were the first to take advantage of the opportunity.

One of the first examples of this was the Obama campaign in 2008. The campaign was groundbreaking in its use of social media to harness the energy of communities of voters and to turn their discontent with a deeply unpopular war and the economic devastation of the global financial meltdown into a call for change. In the words of the campaign, to turn "despair" into "hope." And to do it with a sense of optimism that was captured in the call to arms, "Yes, we can."

The words and phrases that anchored the campaign became iconic as they were designed into posters and T-shirts. The artist Shepard Fairey created one of the most recognizable pieces of street art from the 2000s with his Obama *Hope* poster. Different communities played with the "brand" in different ways. One, for example, was made up of young mothers who literally wore their feelings on their sleeves with T-shirts defining themselves as Obama Mamas.

But the Obama Mamas were just one of many communities that were galvanized by a campaign that sought to "involve your converts and preach to the undecided."

That year, Obama was named *Ad Age's* Marketer of the Year, and the reasons for the win—above more traditional marketers like Nike and Apple—spoke volumes about a different approach to marketing.

One of the award show judges commented, "I think he did a great job of going from a relative unknown to a household name to being a candidate for president." It's difficult now to set our minds back to remember Barack Obama as an unknown senator from Illinois. But unknown he was. And the momentum the campaign created was astonishing at the time.

Another judge commented, "To see what he's done, to be able to create a social network and do it in a way where it's created the tools to let people get engaged very easily. It's very easy for people to participate." And participation was central to the campaign. The Obama Mamas bought and wore T-shirts; countless others bought Shepard Fairey's poster. And—through smart performance marketing—millions of people donated small amounts of money through social channels that, in aggregate, created a massive financial war chest.

A 2008 article by Professor John Quelch in *Harvard Business Review* analyzed the campaign and highlighted a number of tenets that defined its success. Two rise to the top.

Firstly, he was absolutely true to himself and what he stood for.

> Obama's personal charisma... and his compelling biography attracted the attention and empathy of voters. His tone and demeanor throughout the campaign consistently communicated his upbeat themes of hope and "change you can believe in."

The central theme of the campaign never wavered. A focus on hope, progress, and a belief that "Yes, we can" was employed in every communication, in every medium. And that sense of hope and belief in the possible was an entirely believable "truth" coming from the black son of a single white mother who was running for president of the United States. Importantly too, after eight years of foreign wars and an omnipresent threat of terrorism, hope was what the American electorate craved and they too believed that "yes, we can."

And Obama lived that truth, creating iconic and immediately recognizable imagery and words that defined his candidacy and his philosophy. He gave his supporters simple ways to partic-ipate. From buying posters and wearing T-shirts to donating and letter writing, people felt involved and engaged.

> Obama converted this empathy into tangible support...He attracted more donors than the entire Democratic or Republican party nation-wide. Almost half of Obama's unprecedented $639 million in funds raised from individuals came from small donors giving $300 or less.

And second, his campaign got talked about.

> He leveraged his website, the blogosphere, and even user-generated content and video games to engage not just donors and volunteers but all citizens.

> Obama reached out to all citizens. He targeted his message beyond previous or likely voters. He built a coalition that energized young, first-time voters and registered thousands of previous non-voters.

The professor referenced other noteworthy aspects of the Obama marketing machine that apply directly to the art of polit-ical campaigning. But the principles highlighted above describe a foundational shift in the way that successful marketing for any brand, in any category, could (and perhaps should) be employed.

1. Be true to yourself.
2. Get people talking.

In the political sphere, it was next employed by a candidate who sought to distance himself in every way from the stance of Obama. And yet, ironically, much of the campaign-winning playbook that Donald Trump employed in his 2016 presidential run was resonant of the approaches that made Obama a winner eight years earlier.

MAKE AMERICA GREAT
AGAIN—TRUMP 2016

On October 4, 2016, *Marketing Week* wrote: *Donald Trump has rewritten the rules of political communications with a campaign that has earned billions of dollars' worth of free media coverage.*

In the same magazine, the marketing professor Mark Ritson wrote: *The stunning success of Donald Trump's earned media strategy proves that social media and content marketing work when brands are willing to take risks.*[10]

In his analysis, Ritson referenced an article in the *New York Times* that summarized data from a media research group called mediaQuant. The data were startling.

Trump was consistently outspent by all but his most ineffectual competitors. (Through February 2015, Ted Cruz had spent more than double what Trump had on advertising. Jeb Bush had outspent him by 800 percent.)

The distribution of ad spend between candidates was dramatic and led the *Times* to comment that:

> Of all the ways Donald Trump has shocked the
> political system, one of the most significant is how

he wins primary after primary with one of the smallest campaign budgets...Most important, he spent less on television advertising—typically the single biggest expenditure for a campaign—than any other major candidate.[11]

The lack of television advertising was indeed notable. For the last seventy years of the broadcast era, TV advertising—and the big campaign budgets needed to support it—had been an indispensable, almost unquestioned, aspect of every successful political campaign. Without the budgets to pay for a robust TV campaign or the messaging platform to make it effective, political pundits would effectively deem potential candidates unviable. But, in this one of many ways, Trump appeared to be overturning convention. The lack of spending in paid media didn't seem to influence the delivery of his message or the popularity of his campaign. And the answer to why lies in his ability to dwarf his competitors in earned-media reach.

Trump mirrored his competitors' dominance in paid media with his own dominance in earned media. And what was equally clear was that the overall volume of earned media dwarfed that of paid media. And Trump dwarfed his rivals in the proportion of free media he earned—almost 900 percent more than Jeb Bush, for example, his closest republican rival. Again, from the *Times*:

> Like all candidates, he benefits from what is known as earned media: news and commentary about his campaign on television, in newspapers and magazines, and on social media. The big difference between Mr. Trump and other candidates is that he is far better than any other

candidate—maybe than any candidate ever—at earning media.

The Ritson article in *Marketing Week* went on to raise a glass in support of "content marketing and social media" as the driver of Trump's marketing success—and, at the same time, to sound a warning that those tools were best employed by individuals rather than brands. Furthermore, he cautioned that they were best employed by individuals who were naturally fascinating (as opposed to the risk-averse and "inherently boring" world of corporate brand marketing).

Now, there's no doubt that Trump was, and is, fascinating. And that fascinating, provocative, even controversial actions tend to generate media coverage. But perhaps by focusing judgment on just two aspects of earned media—content marketing and social media—the broader point may have been missed: Trump's entire campaign, from conception to execution, was created to maximize the impact of earned media in all forms—social, digital, newspapers, and television. Word of mouth, chatter on forums, conversations in bars, panels on TV shows, celebrity commentary—all of it is media. All of it forms a medium for the delivery of a message. (Even negative commentary amplifies a message.) And, in many ways, all of it was generated by using many of the same principles that had channeled the earned-media conversation toward Obama eight years earlier.

1. Be true to yourself. ⟶ Let Trump Be Trump, Make America Great Again
2. Get people talking. ⟶ The MAGA hat, the Trump flag, and stadium rallies

Interestingly, although Trump was clearly being Trump, it was a version of his "truth" that authentically connected to the cultural moment and to his audience. One objective reality of Trump was that he was the privileged son of a wealthy New York property developer. But he was also an outsider. He grew up in Queens, not in Manhattan. He didn't see himself as part of the political establishment; he wasn't "one of them." In his mind, he was a flag-waving, freedom-loving believer in America First. He was the blue-collar billionaire whose speech was as plain as his disdain for the snowflake wokeness of the Democrats. And in presenting what was, to him, an entirely authentic version of himself, he found a connection with a population who felt sidelined and forgotten, who'd lost their voice and wanted things to be like they used to be. Trump was like them. And the fact that he sat on gold toilets and owned country clubs didn't seem to contradict that.

Both those principles—truth and talkability—built on one another to create a self-reinforcing media hubbub. And that hubbub ultimately led to a political—and marketing—upset that, even in 2024, still had many traditional marketers and politicians scratching their heads, to their chagrin. Because, as the world knows all too well, he did it again.

MAKE AMERICA GREAT AGAIN, AGAIN—TRUMP 2024

Once again, he stayed true to his outsider brand. His blue-collar billionaire demeanor was perfectly exemplified by the paradox and irony of his ability to convince health-obsessed RFK Jr. to enjoy a McDonald's meal for a private jet photo opportunity. (Doesn't everyone eat McDonald's on their private jet?) But this time, his sophisticated manipulation of the media ramped up even further.

In fact, the 2024 general election may have been decided by a podcast.

The Trump campaign had what, in many previous political cycles, might have been the defining moment of an election: the failed assassination attempt in July 2024. The images from that moment—and the defiance and strength they communicated—would have been decisive in any other election campaign. But the news cycle moves fast, and by the time of the Democratic National Convention in mid-August, with Kamala Harris as the new candidate, there was tremendous energy and optimism surrounding the Democratic campaign. (And it was reflected by a corresponding dip in energy from Trump.)

But by October, Trump had signed on as a no-holds-barred guest on the *Joe Rogan Experience*, a podcast reaching fifty million or more listeners a month, most of whom were squarely in Trump's demographic. At the same time, he was attending UFC bouts at Madison Square Garden and had committed to bringing WWE's Linda McMahon into his cabinet. These were unprecedented media moments in a presidential campaign, dwarfing the reach of traditional appearances on broadcast and cable news shows and bringing more outsider energy into the heart of the campaign.

Of course, the Democratic party tried to answer it with an appearance on *Call Her Daddy*, Alex Cooper's provocative podcast, which—while significant in size—has less than half the listeners of Joe Rogan. But talkability is only as powerful as the truth being talked about. And while Trump could be unfiltered and off script, Harris's presentation of her political brand truth failed to resonate.

And one month later, the results were in.

But although politics provides a particularly visible case study of how media and marketing have changed, it isn't the only cultural avenue to have benefited from an alternative approach to marketing.

K-POP AND THE
MAKING OF BTS

There is little question that one of the most impactful—and per-haps surprising—cultural sensations of recent years has been the burgeoning popularity of K-pop, and particularly the industry dominance of the genre's vanguard: BTS.

On an average day, BTS (which doesn't stand for Back to School, but for Bangtan Sonyeondan—Bulletproof Boy Scouts) is mentioned six hundred thousand times on Twitter. In the past ten years, they have sold forty million physical albums (at a time when album sales for musical acts in general are in the dol-drums). They reportedly contribute $5 billion to South Korea's GDP each year.[12]

Importantly, BTS achieved success without the backing of a major American music label or the marketing and promotional infrastructure that goes along with it. Instead, they have dili-gently and purposefully cultivated an army of fans called, funnily enough, ARMY (which stands for Adorable Representative M.C. for Youth).

The mastermind behind their global incursion is Bang Si-hyuk, a songwriter, producer, and founder of Big Hit Entertainment—

the management company behind BTS. "Hitman" Bang, as he is generally known, founded Big Hit in 2005—the dawn of social media—and he has applied the principles of social media expertly ever since. As he told *Time* magazine:

> "It's difficult for me to say things like A led to B," he said. "But what I can say is that BTS' success in the U.S. market was achieved by a formula different from the American mainstream formula. Loyalty built through direct contact with fans had a lot to do with that."[13]

One unusual aspect of the South Korean music industry is that it operates on an apprenticeship basis. Like the system for developing soccer players in Europe, budding stars are selected through regular mass auditions. Once in the "trainee system," they are instructed in all aspects of pop stardom: singing, musicianship, dance, and physical conditioning. Importantly, they are also schooled in developing a social media presence and cultivating a personal brand.

In fact, Big Hit considers supporting an artist's social-media presence and interaction with their fanbase to be one of the most important services it provides to its artists. And the tenets of its approach to cultivating personal brands, once again, echo loudly.

Firstly, bands and individual performers are encouraged to understand what they stand for. To know who they are. And to stick to it.

> Ever since BTS' debut, they've never suddenly switched gears or changed pace. They were consistent. They respect diversity and justice,

the rights of youths and marginalized people.
(Hitman Bang, *Time*)

BTS has been unwavering in communicating their central platform—through their lyrics, their social media activities, and, importantly for them, their philanthropic activities, which have included working directly with the United Nations.

Their central message is to "Love Yourself." With that, they have spoken out about, and engaged their fans on, issues such as LGBTQ rights, self-harm, body image, mental health, and more. Each of those issues is felt more personally by Generation Z—people born between 1996 and 2010, who make up BTS's core demographic—than by any generation that preceded them. (Thirty-five percent of Gen Z say they know someone who uses gender-neutral pronouns, for example, compared to 25 percent of millennials, 16 percent of Gen X, and just 12 percent of boomers.)[14]

So, in much the same way that Donald Trump's truth—that he was a plain-speaking outsider—resonated with a population of Americans who felt disenfranchised and forgotten, BTS connected with a global population of Gen Z who needed to be reminded that they were good, that they would be OK, and that they needed to love themselves.

Unusually perhaps for a group that has been manufactured by a brilliant songwriter, BTS writes many of its own lyrics. They tackle topics like bullying and depression, and they do it with an authenticity that comes from walking in the shoes of their fans. So when they address issues like bullying or self-harm, they do it with a verisimilitude that would be difficult to imagine coming from a middle-aged billionaire like Bang.

This empathy, understanding, and consistency have created an intimacy with their fans that has resonated on a global level. A young fan from Malaysia called Atiqah was interviewed about her passion for the band. She spoke about a troubling time at work: her moods had darkened, her depression had deepened, and then she discovered the song "Tomorrow."

> The song is basically about how we may seem trapped in a cycle of repetition every day, but we can believe that tomorrow will be better," she recalls. "This was it. This song made me [a member of the] ARMY."[15]

It's important to note that the parenthesis here was added by the interviewer, not the interviewee. Atiqah did not say that she became a "member of" ARMY. She said she *became* ARMY.

Participation is central to *being* ARMY. In one record-breaking example of fan engagement, they coordinated mass streaming parties for the debut of the single "Boy with Luv." And in doing so, they crushed the record for the most-viewed YouTube video ever, with close to seventy-five million views in the first twenty-four hours.

But it's not all about clicks and views.

In a familiar show of fandom, the ARMY performs coordinated maneuvers inside concert stadiums. Like soccer fans in Europe, they create and perform complex chants, make banners to represent their cohort, and perform mass, synchronized displays of movement with light sticks. The band constantly fuels this fandom with relentless publishing of social content. Consider this list of social media achievements. BTS was named Top Social Artist at the Billboard Music Awards three years in a row. They became the fastest account to reach one million subscribers on TikTok. (It took three hours and thirty-three minutes.) And band member V claimed the most liked image of all time with 5.8 million likes. (He beat his own record.)

Although BTS operates in the world of popular culture, their commercial success has been enormous—their contribution to South Korea is equal to that of twenty-one mid-size companies. And, once again, many of the modern marketing principles that made Barack Obama and Donald Trump political stars were successfully applied to a different kind of media star.

1. Be true to yourself. ⟶ "Love Yourself."
2. Get people talking. ⟶ Engage the ARMY, win in social media.

BTS, Obama, Trump, Glossier, and Tesla are just a few of the notable commercial, cultural, and political sensations that have been created without reliance on traditional marketing techniques and without access to large paid-media budgets. Like hundreds of other successful brands that have been built in the same period, there are clear principles they have applied to achieve their success.

They understood clearly and unambiguously what they stand for (and what they represent in the minds of their constituents, their fans, or their customers), and they have remained steadfastly true to that intersection between their sense of self and what their audience wants from them. Regardless of the breadth of their appeal, they have been consistent in their message: "Yes, We Can," "Make America Great Again," "Love Yourself," "Skin First, Makeup Second, Smile Always." They have lived that truth, designing their brand experience in a way that makes it easy to participate in their story, however that story may be played out. Their imagery is telegraphic and distinctive. Their rituals are memorable and inviting. Their narrative is consistent. They have invited people to attend rallies, post content, participate in product development, write about them, and review their activities. They have given fuel to their fans. They have nurtured their community.

And they have been tireless in their pursuit of headlines, likes, tweets, shares, and comments, creating palpable energy around their brand. Through traditional and social media, in person and online, they have been an active, almost ubiquitous presence in the lives of the people who care about them.

Whether consciously or unconsciously, all of them have applied a new model to their marketing.

TRUTH AND TALKABILITY

Many of the greatest social, political, cultural, and commercial standouts from the last fifteen years have built their brands and their businesses without relying on traditional broadcast-era marketing approaches and without the paid-media war chests of their competitors. These celebrities, politicians, social movements, and brands surround us every day. The more we look for them, the more of them we see. Talk show hosts like James Corden and Jimmy Fallon. Social movements like Black Lives Matter and The Proud Boys. Politicians like Marjorie Taylor-Greene and Nigel Farage. And most importantly for marketers, a host of modern, digitally native brands that have employed their modus operandi without really thinking there was an alternative—and are enjoying great success as a result. Warby Parker, Casper Mattresses, Uber, Airbnb, and on and on and on.

Instead of broadcast-era marketing approaches and large paid-media war chests, they have relied on branding that stays consistently true to who they are and what they stand for. And brand building that gets talked about, that dances like no one's watching with edgy, stimulating, exciting brand actions that grab headlines and invite discussion, comment, and participation.

Their branding is successful because they are clear on their "truth." They have a clear sense of self and a clear sense of what people look for from them. They know their story, its purpose, and the role they play in the world. They create distinctive brand assets (often created and designed in ways that feel magically enticing). But more importantly, they consistently do things that feel true to their brand. Truth, in their sense of self and in their sense of what people want and expect from them, is at the center of what they do and how they do it.

And their brand building gets people talking. They create tremendous energy around themselves and make it easy for people to participate—to join the party: to chat, to gossip, to comment, to like, to share, to post, to write. They always try to be engaging guests—entertaining, funny, interesting, and newsworthy. The kind of guest that people want to talk about: "Did you hear the story they told?" "Did you see what they were wearing?" "Have you heard who they are going out with?" Their brand building has an implicit talkability to it.

They are true to the brand's sense of self and true to the conception that people have of the brand. And their brand building is implicitly *talkable*—it energetically generates comments and participation.

THE TRUTH AND TALKABILITY MATRIX

We can start to illustrate these points with a simple quadrant chart. We'll put Truth on the Y-axis and Talkability on the X-axis.

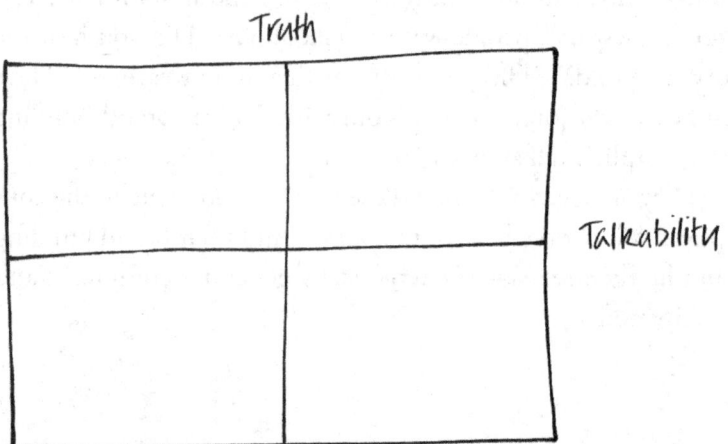

(I know 2x2 matrices are often accused of being oversimplifications of difficult concepts, but I love them—and, in the spirit of this investigation, I am convinced that simplification is one of the factors that leads to talkability. Also, if you're interested, read Noah Brier's defense of the 2x2 matrix on his brilliant Substack, *Why is this interesting?*[16])

So here goes, as with all quadrant charts, the absolute best place to be is the upper right-hand square: the most truthful activity with the most talkable actions. It is where brands like Tesla and Glossier, politicians like Obama and Trump, and cultural forces like BTS all consistently land. In this quadrant, powerful actions lead to powerful brands.

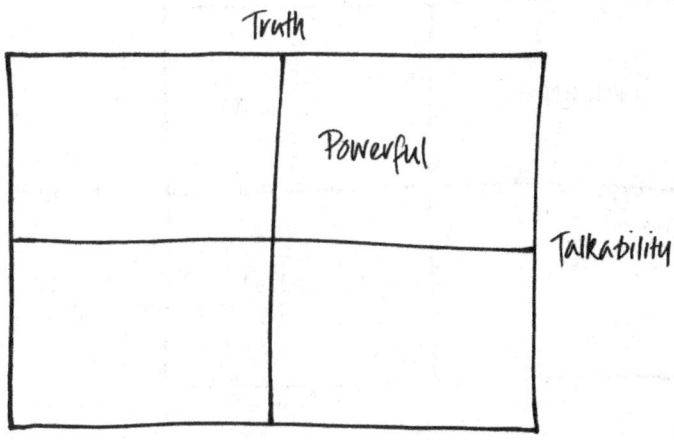

Equally, it becomes easy to plot where less successful brands have gone wrong. To take Trump's political rivals (and to dramatically oversimplify for effect): Biden—although steadfastly true to his principles—did nothing to create talkable excitement around his policies or his many achievements. Conversely, Harris had a talkable energy and significant momentum but was unable to articulate the central truth that defined her campaign or her candidacy.

The benefit of a simple model like the Truth and Talkability matrix is that it clearly highlights issues that need to be fixed and suggests how best to fix them. (At the end of the book, I'll look at examples of campaigns that fall into different quadrants of the matrix and what can be done to fuel them or fix them.) In the upper left and lower right quadrants—Biden and Harris, respectively—the brands have potential but need to refocus.

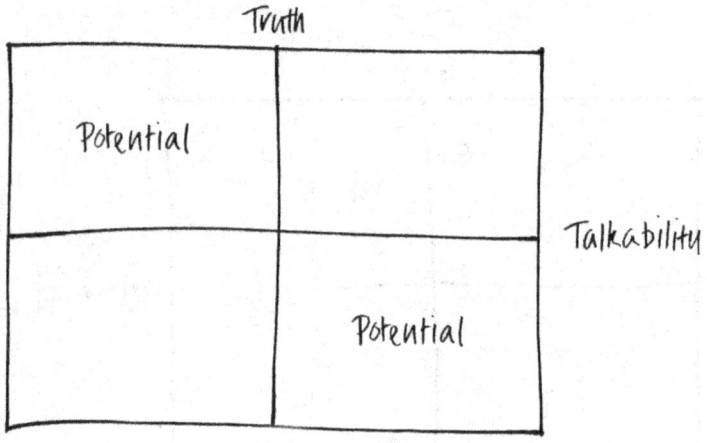

At this point, it probably goes without saying that brands—or brand actions—that find themselves in the bottom left quadrant should be immediately ceased or shot down.

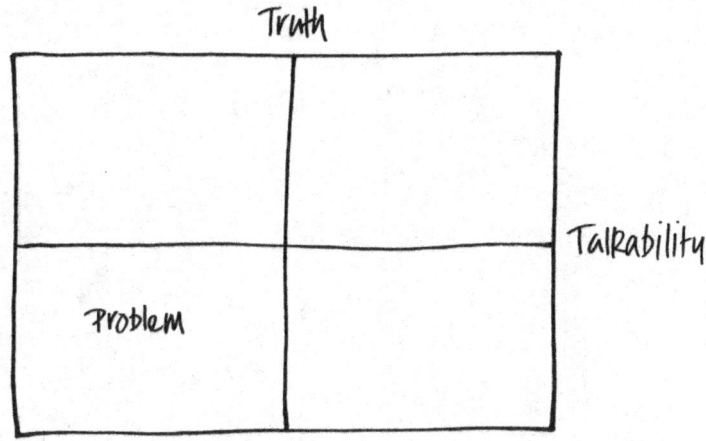

Importantly, although simple, these principles—and the success stories they've created—are consistent with long-standing marketing theory. But although they've worked to the same theoretical principles as brands that grew in the broadcast era (whether consciously or unconsciously), they haven't used the executional principles of broadcast-era marketing. So, what are those principles, and how are modern brands and cultural success stories executing against them?

PART THREE

A NEW MARKETING MODEL

"The ultimate aim of marketing is
to make selling superfluous."

(PETER DRUCKER)

MARKETING EVOLUTION

"Only in marketing do we attempt to knock down our theoretical cathedrals and replace them with rapidly inflated bouncy castles that smell of piss." (Mark Ritson)[17]

My layman's understanding of the evolutionary process is that it is a search for balance between maintaining a comfortable status quo and responding to an environmental or cultural need for change. Take the giraffe.

A long time ago, it had a short neck. And it would have been quite happy plodding around, munching the occasional leaf, had it not been for the fact that long-necked giraffes attracted the opposite sex. (The long necks helped them reach higher leaves, which aided their prospects of survival, which is quite attractive in a giraffe.) So, the evolutionary principle kicked in, and long-necked giraffes begot longer-necked giraffes.

But the necks could only get so long. There would come a point at which they wouldn't be able to lift their heads to eat or run fast from predators. And so, balance was reached: necks that were attractively long but functional.

In the marketing world, there is a very clear environmental and cultural need for change. The tools of broadcast-era marketing just aren't as efficient as they once were. We're paying more money for smaller audiences, we're consuming more media but seeing less advertising, and marketing budgets are being diverted to the bottom of the sales funnel, leaving brand building at the top unsupported and underdone. But in many cases, we appear to be more comfortable maintaining the status quo than changing our marketing approaches to reflect a changed media and cultural environment. When, in fact, if we reshaped our approach to marketing and communication to reflect those cultural shifts, we could gain some level of evolutionary advantage over our competitors.

Now, it's important to state here that I'm not suggesting we recklessly abandon all aspects of the traditional marketing playbook. There is no revolutionary zeal here. And there is a clear-eyed recognition that many of the most modern of the digitally native brands have used broadcast-era marketing tools to build their businesses. Amazon, notably, is now one of the largest advertisers in the world, for example. But while we certainly don't want to stretch our necks out too far in rethinking our approaches to marketing, it's probably best to avoid plodding along and munching on low-hanging leaves.

So, to think about the evolution from broadcast-era marketing to marketing in the Attention Economy, let's avoid throwing the baby out with the bathwater—and hold on to the unchanging fundamentals that underpin the discipline.

THE FUNDAMENTAL "LAW" OF MARKETING

Understanding how modern marketers are building modern brands really requires us to think about the fundamentals of how brands are built at all. And that, of course, is a Holy Grail question—hotly debated, much theorized, and full of conjecture, opinion, and anecdote.

A one-time boss of mine, a very smart and senior executive, rejected the idea that anyone knew the answer, going so far as to state with regularity that "there are no right answers in marketing." And, frankly, there was an appealing truth to that statement. Marketing (and particularly the long-term brand-building part of it) relies on a creative alchemy that connects a brand's delivery to a consumer's desire. And saying that there's a right or wrong way to do that would be a little naïve (much as some advertising research companies would have you believe otherwise).

However, for all the attractive nuance contained in that simple statement, it does belie the fact that there are (a few) rights and (probably a lot of) wrongs in marketing. There are repeatable—even, dare I utter the word, "empirical"—principles of marketing that explain how people choose brands and buy products.

Marketing is a social science and, as such, concerns itself with the messy world of people: their minds, how they respond to stimuli, how they remember things, and what attracts them to A rather than B. It's a murky world, and the murkiness precludes us from enjoying the precision of laws that apply in the physical sciences—clear, predictable laws that determine how quickly apples fall from trees.

But there are predictable patterns in marketing. Behaviors that can be modeled more or less accurately and that describe the way people, in the aggregate, buy things. (While they may not be "laws" in the purest sense, they are very close cousins.)

The observation and discussion of these patterns and principles have become very popular over the last few years. What was once a slow-moving tributary in the river of business thinking has become a veritable whitewater. Much of that is due to the echo chamber of LinkedIn, which has created an outlet and an audience for snackable thought pieces on the theory of marketing. But much more is due to the sterling work of a few notable writers who have succeeded in illuminating many of the principles that had been hitherto ignored. Chief among them is Byron Sharp, who wrote the fabulously digestible *How Brands Grow*, but also folks like Les Binet and Peter Field, who are inexhaustible in their marketing data pattern spotting, and Paul Feldwick, who has both chronicled popular theories of how advertising works and established his own perspective on fame. Each of them (and several others) has pushed the field of marketing forward. But all of them have built their houses on the foundations of one man's thinking: a certain Professor Andrew Ehrenberg.

MCPHEE, EHRENBERG, AND DOUBLE JEOPARDY

I would argue that the most important phrase in the new lexicon of marketing thinking is the beautifully simple statement: "Market share is driven by popularity."

That elegant quote is from *How Brands Grow* by Byron Sharp.[18] The book has developed a slightly cult-like devotion from corporate marketers since it was published in 2010, which is slightly ironic because the foundational research that the book is built on has been in the public domain since the 1960s.

Popularity as a driver of market share is a law—or at least law-like. It is not an intuition, a provocation, or an assertion. It can be accurately modeled. It is repeatable across products, categories, and countries. It is supported by data collected over the course of the last sixty years or so. There is at least one right answer in marketing, and that is the answer to the question: "What drives market share?" The answer is popularity.

The importance of that concept is difficult to overstate. So, to reinforce it, it's worth digging into the basis for it.

In 1963, a sociologist from Columbia University named William McPhee noticed something he found a little unfair.

While researching the popularity of Hollywood actors, he saw that those who were most popular were also liked more than those who were less popular. He found it counterintuitive and a little troubling that actors who spent their lives perfecting their craft rather than chasing the blockbuster movie not only enjoyed smaller fan bases but were also, ultimately, loved less by the fans they did have.

He went on to research the effect in different forms of media and found the same pattern. Radio programs that were listened to by large numbers of people were also listened to more regularly by those people. Once again, slightly counterintuitive. One might think, for example, that a program about fly fishing that didn't manage to attract a mainstream audience would at least be enjoyed more passionately by those who enjoyed "the contemplative man's recreation." But sadly, and empirically, it's not true.

The same applied to comic strips: the big, popular ones were not only read by more people than the smaller, more artful, more insightful comics but were also liked more by their readers.

Troubled by this pattern (and perhaps leaning toward the liberal in his politics), McPhee named it Double Jeopardy. Not only were the smaller players liked by fewer people, but they were also liked less by those few who liked them...

FROM DOUBLE JEOPARDY TO DOUBLE AWESOME

Later in the decade, the British academic Professor Andrew Ehrenberg read McPhee's research and asked himself whether the law of Double Jeopardy could be applied to consumer buying behavior. Rather than simply liking popular brands more, would people put their money where their like was and buy those brands more?

So, he set out to study the effect and repeatedly saw that the most popular brands were not only bought by more people but were also bought more often by those people.

Ehrenberg, being the diligent statistician he was, went on to model the dynamic. He studied categories ranging from shampoo and household detergent all the way to airline oil contracts. And not only did he see that the law held true, but he also found that he could predict it.

The model, called the "NBD-Dirichlet model of brand choice" (catchy), demonstrated that a brand's penetration (the number of people who buy it) correlated perfectly with its repeat purchase rate (the number of times they buy it) in an entirely predictable way.

Big brands were indeed bought by more people, but they were also bought more often than before. So, for example, around seventy million people buy food from McDonald's every day and those people buy food 3.1 times per month on average. Burger King has eleven million daily visitors and people buy from them 1.7 times per month. The bigger brand is bought by more people and is bought more often by those people.

That double punch means that big brands are exponentially bigger than small brands. In fact, if you plot the brands in any category on a graph with their market share on the Y axis and their market leadership ranking on the X axis, you see a consistent pattern.

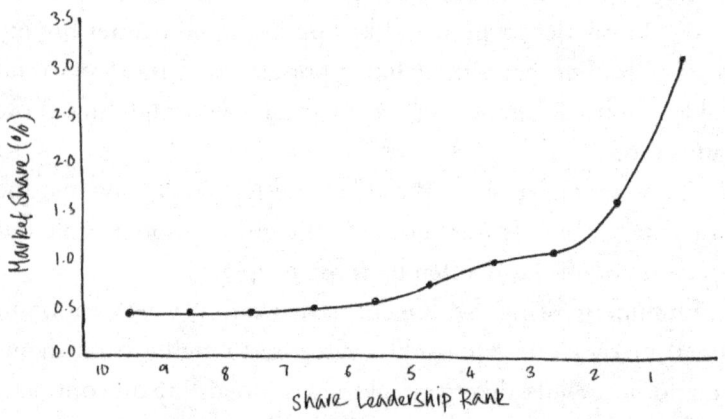

Somewhere along the line, toward the right-hand side of the graph, there is a marked uptick in trajectory. The line heads sharply toward the sky. The shape is called an exponential growth curve, and it describes what it says on the tin.

Big brands aren't just proportionately bigger than small brands. Big brands are exponentially bigger than small brands.

Talk about double awesome!

Once again, the effect is predictable and repeatable. Big beer brands are exponentially bigger than small beer brands. Big soda brands are exponentially bigger than small soda brands. Big shampoo brands are exponentially bigger than small shampoo brands. And on, and on, and on...

When you understand the dynamic, you can play a game with it. Sales and usage data are regularly reported in the business press, and when you see numbers of buyers, or listeners, or readers of one brand in relation to one of its competitors, you can predict the volume of repeat purchases or repeat viewing or repeat listening. (An excellent trick for parties—or at least an excellent trick for slightly dull parties.)

The implications of this finding for marketing and marketers are stunning. We have a repeatable law of purchase behavior at our fingertips. A law, mind you. Not the guesswork or statistical skullduggery that often guides the practice of marketing—a gosh darn law. (OK, it's just law-like, but, hell, that's progress.)

And then something funny happened.

Everyone ignored it.

In fairness, far fewer people are ignoring Ehrenberg's work now than they were in 2011. Thanks to Byron Sharp and his colleagues at the Ehrenberg-Bass Institute, Ehrenberg's findings have become a great deal more digestible in recent years.

Not so early on. As brilliant as he was, Ehrenberg was, ironically, not a skilled marketing man. His practical grasp of branding was weak. Witness this definition of a Dirichlet model from Wikipedia:

> A family of continuous multivariate probability distributions parameterized by a vector of positive reals. It is a multivariate generalization of the beta distribution, hence its alternative name of **multivariate beta distribution (MBD)**. Dirichlet distributions are commonly used as prior distributions in Bayesian statistics, and in fact the Dirichlet distribution is the conjugate prior of the categorical distribution and multinomial distribution.

What?

The slightly sad truth is that Ehrenberg's research is pretty impenetrable if you don't love math. (Guilty...) This, in itself, might not have consigned the law of Double Jeopardy to the marketing wasteland had it not been for the fact that, at the same time Ehrenberg was doing his fancy calculations, another very famous marketing professor (in a bigger market with a bigger fan base, funnily enough) was popularizing the concept of brand loyalty.

Philip Kotler is called the "father of marketing." He published *Marketing Management* in 1991, now in its fifteenth edition.[19] *Marketing Management* became the de facto totem of marketing education, and likely anyone who completed an MBA from the 1990s until now has Kotler to thank for their understanding of marketing.

Kotler doesn't talk about popularity driving market share in his tome. He doesn't reference Double Jeopardy or the Dirichlet model of brand choice. Instead, he writes about Brand Loyalty, Lifetime Value, and loyalty programs. And those things conflict with the law of Double Jeopardy and the idea that popularity drives market share.

Now, he wasn't the first person to speak to the idea of Brand Loyalty. That distinction goes to Jacoby and Chestnut,[20] who wrote a book about it in 1978, just when Ehrenberg was in the thick of his research. But it's probably fair to say that Kotler locked the idea into the minds of professional marketers.

And in one of the great ironies of our industry, a law that explained the power of popularity in driving market share was confined to the scrapheap by an idea that was more popular.

SO, WHAT ABOUT LOYALTY?

The strength of the idea of brand loyalty is that it's intuitive. It makes sense. It's human. Its weakness is that there is no data to support it. It is intuitive. It is not empirical.

Now, it's clear that loyalty matters in many parts of our lives. Loyalty absolutely matters in relationships, for example. One hopes for loyalty from their partner or their spouse. We're loyal to our family, our friends, our colleagues, our brothers in arms. Some of us may be loyal to a sports team (although the data is questionable on that). We may be loyal to a country or flag (but, as a Scotsman with an American passport, I can attest that even that loyalty can be divided). But beyond that, are we loyal to things? Specifically, can we really be loyal to brands?

If, as Kotler and most people who studied him do, we believe that we can be loyal to brands, there is an enormous temptation to create marketing programs specifically to increase that loyalty and sell more things to the same group of people. *All we need to do is get all our customers to buy one more bar of chocolate (can of soda, T-shirt, burrito) per year, and we will smash our objectives! It's just one more, you guys!*

Whole categories focus significant portions of their money and effort on those programs. And whole marketing disciplines have grown up around them. But the data would suggest that much of that money and effort is wasted.

When we boil it all down, there is only one ultimate measure of success in marketing, and that is sales. And there are only two components to sales: penetration (how many people buy it) and repeat purchase (how often they buy it). We can either focus on selling to more people or on selling more things to the same people.

As an industry, we tend to believe that to achieve the former, we need to increase popularity, and to achieve the latter, we need to increase loyalty. And that is where we go wrong. Because, as Ehrenberg found categorically, the only way to increase repeat purchase is to increase penetration. Or, put another way, the only way to create more "loyalty" is to create more popularity.

Back to that idea of playing games when you see data on a brand's penetration reported in the business press. At the end of 2019, Spotify's paid-subscriber base reached 113 million, compared to Apple Music's 60 million paid subscribers. At the same time (unsurprisingly to Ehrenberg fans), their engagement rates were higher too. As a spokesperson said,

> Relative to Apple, the publicly available data shows that we are adding roughly twice as many subscribers per month as they are. Additionally, we believe that our monthly engagement is roughly 2x as high and our churn is at half the rate.[21]

More users for Spotify also created more usage per user. The data is consistently clear. And yet even smart global marketers fall into the trap of feeling intuitively that we are loyal to certain brands. But are we? Really?

An article recently referenced some of the mistakes Adidas had made in marketing investment:

> At the same time, Adidas brought in an econometric model. That helped it discover that where it had thought loyal customers were driving sales, and it was therefore investing in CRM, in fact 60% of revenue came from first-time buyers.[22]

The primary implication for marketing is to think less about last click and more about first principles.

If people don't know about your brand, they can't buy it. Our focus as marketers should be to think consistently about what will make us more popular. Because yes, loyalty matters—particularly loyalty to the people around us. But it can't be created for brands—other than by selling those brands to more people. And that only happens when we make our brands more popular.

POPULARITY IN THE
ATTENTION ECONOMY

Popularity is the lifeblood of the Attention Economy. In many ways, it makes more sense as a business and marketing concept now than it did during the broadcast era.

The idea of popularity fits neatly with the practice of tweeting and TikToking. It is a self-evident aspect of celebrity culture. Popularity is a fundamental driver of the influencer business. But popularity is an interesting word. We all know what it means. We may have benefited from it, or struggled with it, in high school. We can all apply it to things in our lives. But I will place a firm bet on the fact that few of us ever think particularly deeply about it—or indeed wonder at what alchemy creates it. But if brand growth is driven by popularity, then wonder we must.

According to the *Cambridge English Dictionary*—and who are we to argue with them—popularity is "the fact that someone or something is liked, enjoyed or supported by many people." In this context, we're largely concerned with the "some*thing*"— what makes brands popular—although it is important to note that the same principles should be able to be applied to "some*one*"—what makes people popular.

Even in this very simple definition, there are two parts. One is the "liking" (or enjoyment or support) of a person or a thing. And the other is the scale of that liking—the "many people" piece. We can all point to someone or something disliked by many people; this widespread dislike is the thing that makes them deeply unpopular. And conversely, we can point to people or things that are liked, but by very few people, and that generally defines them as "quirky" or "interesting." To be popular is to be liked—and to be liked by many people.

This may seem a little pedantic, but it's important to dwell on because it's not simply enough to be exposed to many people or to be known to many people. And yet it is the volume of exposure rather than the quality of that exposure that is the focus for many traditional marketers.

And perhaps that was understandable when a brand could guarantee that "many people" would be exposed to its marketing or advertising because it could pay for access to a captive audience. But, once again, that's no longer the case.

For most of the last seventy years, marketers have been able to rely on large, receptive audiences for their commercial messages. In the UK (where I grew up), people used to actively like advertising. Many people thought that the advertising was better (smarter, more entertaining) than the scripted programming. People would talk about new campaigns at school and at work. But they don't do that anymore.

As pointed out earlier, a full 47 percent of us skip advertising when we can (that number rises to 82 percent for Gen Z). And consumers pay media owners $1.5 trillion more than advertisers do so we can avoid watching advertising. There are very few captive audiences left for marketers, and consequently, they must think differently about what might engage audiences that are free and fleeting.

To take one random but memorable example, the thing people liked most and were talking about at school and at work at the end of 2020 was a TikTok video of Nathan Apodaca (Doggface) riding his longboard down a highway while sipping Ocean Spray cranberry juice and miming to a forty-five-year-old Fleetwood Mac song.

The video was viewed tens of millions of times in its original form. More than that, it was shared, reposted, and commented on many millions of times more. Joe Rogan featured the video on his podcast. Mick Fleetwood surprised Nathan on a broadcast news program. And thousands of people memed the video. Ocean Spray's response demonstrated perfect attention-economy instincts. Realizing that Nathan was on his board because his truck had broken down, they gave him a new truck. That video was viewed fourteen million times in the first two weeks.

By comparison, Ocean Spray has anchored its advertising with two "Ocean Spray guys" who stand in a cranberry bog and regale viewers with humorous skits. It was by no means "bad" advertising, but no one talks about it, no one tweets about it, or rushes to share new ads with their pals. (The commercial that introduced Ocean Spray SodaStream, for example, racked up nine hundred thousand views over the course of seven years—that's not a lot.) Conversely, platforms like TikTok have created unprecedented mechanisms for cultural transmission, where a single unplanned moment can create more brand value than months of traditional advertising campaigns. We still like content. We even like content that features brands. But, in general, we don't like being sold to, and very often, that's what traditional marketing feels like.

And for good reason. The basic mindset of the traditional marketer is that of the salesperson. Oversimplifying for the sake of clarity, the traditional marketing mindset was to deliver the "reasons to believe" that product X is better than product Y and then to repeat those facts over and over to a captive audience. But we're not captive any longer. This creates something of a marketing conundrum because, although content is consumed and processed differently now than it was in the heyday of advertising, marketers are often approaching their jobs with a perspective on marketing and brand building that is rooted in the practices of the broadcast era. And that does not lend itself to creating popularity. On the contrary, it can often create the impression of a slightly creepy intrusion. It doesn't make your brand liked and certainly doesn't make it liked by a lot of people.

To create popularity in the Attention Economy requires not just a new marketing model but also a clear shift in marketing mindset—from marketer as salesperson to marketer as entertainer.

Which is precisely what successful modern brands like Tesla, Glossier, Trump, Obama, and BTS have done. They have focused their marketing efforts with laser precision on being popular, whether that's Tesla tying one of its Roadsters to a rocket and launching it into space or Trump guesting on the Joe Rogan podcast or showing up at UFC fights. Not simply seen or heard—they could achieve that with traditional marketing approaches—but popular and liked—part of the cultural discourse. And they have done it by applying a new marketing model to their businesses and brands.

AN UNINTENDED
ECONOMIC EXPERIMENT

I suppose it's human nature for us to think most creatively when things seem most dire. If we're wedged in a canyon without food or water, we start to think fast and laterally about how to make our escape. (Even if it means hacking off our arm with an old penknife—on one level, that seems like a terrible idea, but someone did it…and they're still alive.) So perhaps it shouldn't be a surprise that large-scale economic crises result in large-scale commercial innovation.

Just as the global pandemic spurred a wave of innovation in blockchain and digital currencies, the Metaverse (or, more accurately, metaverses—there are many more than one), and AI, the global economic meltdown in 2007–2008 saw a gold rush of innovation around the emerging mobile/social web: web 2.0.

Thousands of businesses arose from it. Many have managed to stand the test of time. Some have become household names; some have even become the generic term for their category (in the same way Kleenex is the generic term for tissues, even though it is just one brand among many brands of tissues). Now, when we car share, we Uber; when we house share, we get an Airbnb—regardless of which brand is delivering the service.

Like Uber and Airbnb, some of these emerging brands were providing a new consumer infrastructure. Others were providing consumer goods to compete with traditional manufacturers. Rhone and Vuori were competing in the athletic apparel market against established competitors like Nike and Under Armour. Glossier was competing in the beauty category against L'Oréal. Warby Parker was competing in eyewear against Ray-Ban. Mattress brands like Saatva and Casper were competing against Tempur-Pedic and Sealy.

Importantly, though, they all chose a new playing field to compete on. This cohort made up the first wave of truly native digital marketers. They hadn't grown up in a traditional marketing background where power lay with national retailers. They were selling directly to consumers through e-commerce, and to do so, they focused less on traditional metrics like share of market, share of category, share of voice, share of mind, and share of wallet.

They were competing for your attention. They were competing for share of culture.

As digital natives, performance marketing was second nature to them. Their grasp of search engine optimization (SEO) and search engine marketing (SEM) was intuitive—and amazingly efficient and profitable. They were natural email marketers. They clearly understood the practice and benefits of targeting and retargeting their digital advertising.

But central to their success was their ability to quickly become part of the zeitgeist, part of the cultural conversation. And they did it by embracing a new set of marketing tools and using them in new ways.

They were making themselves famous with entertaining digital content that was passed from friend to friend because it was fun to watch. They were finding provocative ways to show up in real life—like mattress companies delivering beds on the back of bicycles. They were nurturing and celebrating their fans, their community, by actively engaging with them in real time. They showed up consistently and told their story with passion and consistency.

Somewhere along the line, one of these brilliant (but unsung) digital natives developed a simple model to help think about the totality of the digital media tools they were employing. It was the OESP (or PESO) model, the acronym referencing the various types of media available to those marketers (Owned, Earned, Shared, and Paid). Paid media included digital advertising, paid influencer engagements, and so on. Earned media referenced positive word of mouth, likes, and comments—primarily from social networks but also in forums. Shared media referenced the media benefit arising from partnerships with influencers or other brands. And owned media defined the brand's website, email list, and social media channels, for example.

The OESP model quickly became the lingua franca of digital marketing. And it is probably one of the most recognizable, memorable, and universally accepted concepts in marketing now. The model, as originally conceived, is presented as a Venn diagram, with each of the media types being viewed as having equal importance.

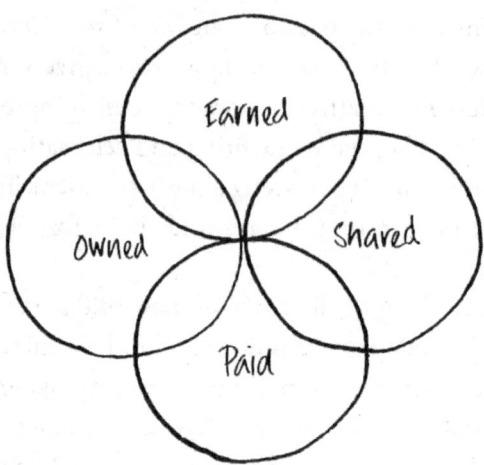

The owned-media bubble is the same size as the earned-media bubble. The earned-media impressions from reviews and word of mouth are viewed as equivalent to impressions from paid digital advertising.

But, interestingly, whereas the democracy of media may have seemed self-evident to those early digital media thinkers, it is very different from the conception of media priority that traditional marketers employ.

In the traditional marketing mindset, there is a firmly established hierarchy. Paid media sits atop the pyramid. The effect of earned and owned media is considered, but rarely to the same degree as the paid media effect is scrutinized. And shared media is barely given a passing thought.

Paid media advertising has been the foundation upon which the marketing ecosystem of the last seventy years has been built. And yet, at least for those digital marketers, paid media was not their sole focus. They were building their brands and businesses in new ways. They didn't rely wholly on paid media as their path to market. In fact, many of them didn't rely on "traditional" paid media at all (the historically effective but notoriously difficult-to-measure combination of TV, print, outdoor, and radio advertising). Their paid media budgets were directed toward the easy-to-measure performance media that defined digital marketing: search engine marketing, digital display advertising, email marketing, and so on. They built their long-term brands through a combination of earned, shared, and owned media.

That simple shift in media prioritization created an incredible, though often overlooked, shift in the way brands and businesses have developed since the mainstreaming of social media in the late 2000s and early 2010s.

As those modern marketing vanguards matured, they recognized that the OESP model had application beyond the digital environment: that their storefronts, showrooms, and catalogs were, in fact, forms of owned media and were powerful brand-building opportunities; that media relations and experiential marketing were powerful ways to use earned media to build the popularity and fame of their brands; and that the media they shared through sponsorships and brand ambassadors were powerful force multipliers for their brand message.

And through that experimentation, a new model for marketing success started to emerge.

Use paid media for short-term performance marketing. Use earned, shared, and owned media to build the long-term brand.

A MODERN
MARKETING MODEL

This new marketing model recognizes the practical fact that paid media investment must necessarily focus on driving performance media and marketing. Marketers simply can't afford to do otherwise. Shopping carts must be optimized. Google must be paid. And even with unlimited money, the cost of paid media continues to increase as the audience for it becomes ever smaller. The job of building the brand and optimizing the top of the funnel, therefore, lands with a combination of owned, earned, and shared media activities.

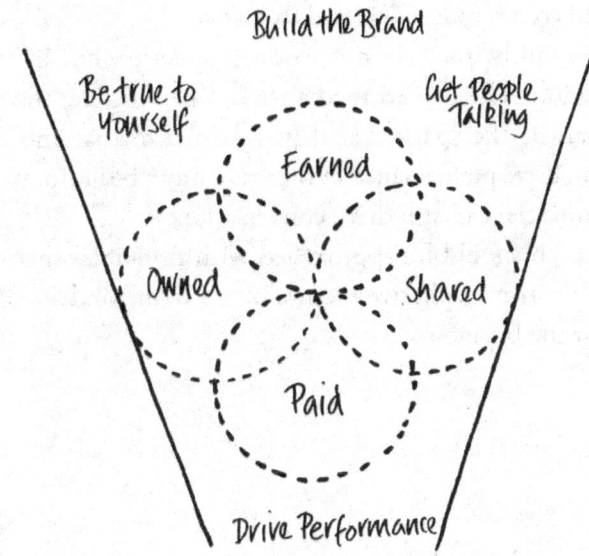

Each of those media has a primary role to play in brand building.

Owned media is where the brand's truth is defined, articulated, and manifested. Through words and images, design, video, and music, the brand is brought to life in a way that is immediate, telegraphic, and distinctive.

Shared media is where the fans find their fuel. In forums, on social channels, at events, through influencer partnerships, fans learn their language, they celebrate their rituals, and commune with each other.

Earned media is the conversation driver, the amplifier, the echo chamber. Earned media is where the brand dances like no one's watching with full and complete understanding of what it is and what it stands for and with zero Fx&!s to give. It is where the world comes to know it and to love it.

Importantly, they do not work in isolation but in studied coordination. The owned media should be talkable; the shared media can be the spark that drives earned media; and earned media can drive performance in the same way a beautifully crafted TV commercial can still drive conversation.

But each should be approached with principles that ensure the whole forms a cohesive picture of the brand and an effective driver for the business.

PART FOUR

APPLYING
THE MODEL

"Be yourself. Everyone else is taken."

(OSCAR WILDE)

FIND YOUR TRUTH

The Need for Brand Truth

The idea of searching for a brand's truth may sound a little lofty or abstract—particularly, I would imagine, to a marketer who has grown up with a traditional "marketing as salesmanship" view of business. But in each of the cases and examples we have looked at so far, it is a central, foundational aspect of their appeal and their popularity. The reasons for that can be seen very clearly if, again, we think about marketing evolution rather than revolution and examine some first principles—starting with Ehrenberg (or at least with Byron Sharp from the Ehrenberg Bass Institute).

As we've established, the fundamental law of marketing is that popularity drives growth.

Say it with me...popularity drives growth.

And when Byron Sharp writes about growing popularity, he focuses on the concept of availability—making a brand accessible to as many people as possible. He breaks the idea of availability into two component parts: physical availability and mental availability. (I'm going to touch on both here, but it's worth a read of Chapter 12 of the excellent *How Brands Grow* if you're interested in a deeper dive.)

Physical Availability

The physical availability of a product is a centrally important aspect of marketing, but something that is perhaps taken for granted by people who spend their lives promoting brands rather than distributing them. The reason for its importance is that, as people, we're not as discerning as we'd like to think. Often, we'll settle for good enough rather than perfect. Generally, we'll have a few brands in our consideration set for anything we need to buy, and we tend to think that there is very little difference between those brands.

This is particularly true of heavy users of a category. A mother with triplets, for example, will buy the brand of diapers (nappies) that she can find in the store she's in rather than leaving and going to another store to buy the ones she has a slight preference for. She needs them now, it's easier, and the differences between the brands are small. So, the simple truth is that, often, you buy what you can find—and vice versa: you don't buy what you can't find.

On that basis, it's tempting to think of physical availability as a fifty-dollar way of saying "distribution." But it's a little more complicated than that. Breadth of distribution is important: "How many stores is the brand in?" But so too is the depth of distribution: "How easy is it to find the brand within the store?" "How many SKUs are being carried?" and "How much shelf space does the brand have?" The answers to those questions determine a brand's physical availability—how much presence it has, how prominent it is in the retail environment, and how relevant the SKUs that are carried are. (I'm using consumer brands in brick-and-mortar retail as an easy-to-explain example here, but the same principle applies for everything from hotels to software manufacturers, and for digital as well as physical environments.)

In digital environments, marketing has a broader role to play in creating physical availability than it does in physical environments. Optimizing search is the first step to creating physical availability in digital environments, and that responsibility (and that cost) tends to land with marketing and the marketing budget now (which, as we have touched on, is creating its own problems). Paying to optimize placement on Amazon or Walmart. com lies with the marketing organization, and it's becoming ever more important and ever more expensive, also creating problems. And shoppable advertising on Facebook, Instagram, or Pinterest is clearly a marketing responsibility and equally clearly a component of physical availability.

It's difficult to overstate the importance of creating physical availability. And it's important to note the increasing involvement of marketing and communications in driving that availability. But there is a very large component of physical availability that lies beyond the scope of the marketing and communications group—most notably, supply chain management, the physical getting of product from manufacturer to consumer. That is something that marketing can't influence or control. (And as we have learnt from the COVID-19 lockdown, and our apparent inability to ship products from point A to point B, it's sometimes something that no one in the organization can fully control.) On the other hand, creating mental availability is the sole responsibility of the marketing and communications organization, so I'll spend a little more time on that.

Mental Availability

Sharp defines mental availability as:

> The probability that a buyer will notice, recognize and/or think of a brand in buying situations. It depends on the quality and quantity of memory structures related to the brand.[23]

Sharp suggests that those memory structures are created through a network of brand associations that the consumer holds about the brand. In one example, he references the associations between McDonald's, hamburgers, fast food, and golden arches. And in referencing these networks of associations, he makes it clear that mental availability is more than simple brand awareness. In his conception, brand awareness—of the brand name or the brand's logo—becomes a single association and, therefore, doesn't predict or suggest the richness of memory structures.

Although he doesn't reference the source, Sharp's explanation of memory being made up of networks of associations is very similar to a theory of memory proposed by Marvin Minsky, the co-founder of the artificial intelligence lab at MIT.[24]

Minsky proposed that memory was created by "K-Lines," that whenever we have a memorable experience, or we have developed an idea or solved a problem, we would begin a K-Line to help us remember the experience, idea, or solution. And he suggests that all the "mental agencies" (sights, sounds, facts, concepts) that were active at the time would attach themselves to this K-Line, so when it was reactivated later, all those agencies would activate along with it.

We would remember not just the event but also the facts and feelings associated with the event.

In his view of memory creation, Minsky recognizes that "attitudes really do precede propositions. Feelings come before facts." (And I would add that the conceptual comes before the concrete.) We make decisions not by *thinking* about them very hard at all but by acting in a way that is consistent with our *feelings* toward a brand.

This perspective is consistent with the thinking of advertising practitioner turned academic Robert Heath, who advanced the view that advertising works not by rational persuasion but by embedding concepts, images, and ideas about a brand into our long-term memory.

He wrote a book called *The Hidden Power of Advertising*,[25] where he examined the effectiveness of a specific advertising campaign (one that he worked on as an advertising planner) for a European beer called Stella Artois. The campaign was famous and successful for many years in the UK but broke all the "rules" of advertising persuasion.

There were no rational messages in the advertising. In fact, it toyed with the (negative) fact that the beer cost a lot more money than domestic brews. The advertisements didn't speak to the product quality of the beer or its brewing process; they simply sought to entertain the audience with skits built around the premise of the beer being "reassuringly expensive."

Heath posited that rather than trying to embed facts about a brand in the rational part of our brains, the neocortex (the frontal lobe that processes those facts but only holds on to them for a very short amount of time), the real effect of advertising was the gradual buildup of favorable images in the limbic system of our brain (the "emotional" brain that processes images and concepts and holds on to those for a very long time).

Heath's view coincided with a raft of research and writing that changed our understanding of the human brain and how we make decisions. We began to realize that we aren't rational actors who make purposeful, calculated decisions—"I think, therefore I am." Rather, we are fundamentally emotional creatures who often make decisions with little rational thought, relying more on what we perceive as our "gut."

We are led by emotion. Our decision-making is subconscious. More than that, in fact—it's pre-cognitive. Prehistoric, even.

Dissecting the Triune Brain

The brain is made up of three distinct parts. The first, and oldest, is the reptilian brain. It's connected directly to our spinal column. It navigates basic bodily functions and moderates the fight-or-flight mechanism.

Surrounding the reptilian brain is the limbic system. This is the area of the brain that we, as marketers and communicators, should focus most of our efforts on understanding. The limbic system manages implicit learning (everything we don't get from a book or a classroom, essentially). It also controls our emotions and feelings. It is where our long-term memories are stored. Importantly, the same part of the brain that controls those troublesome emotions and stores our long-term memories also guides our decision-making.

The third part of the brain is the neocortex. It surrounds both the reptilian brain and the limbic system. It's the human brain. It governs language and reason. It controls short-term memory—the storage of facts. It's what enables us to think. And as a result, we've tended to pay a great deal of attention to this more sophisticated aspect of our minds. But there are limitations to the neocortex. One is that it can't act in isolation. Before the neocortex is involved in any mental process, the reptilian and limbic brains have already been engaged. We can't turn that off, and they fire in sequence—from oldest to newest.

The triune brain evolved, and evolution is messy. The wiring in our brain isn't logical. Although we spend a great deal of time trying to understand how people think, the limbic brain dominates our neocortex. Our feelings are more powerful than our thoughts in determining our actions. (And our fight-or-flight mechanism—*is that thing going to bite me?*—is the most powerful of all.)

The simple truth is that thought follows feeling, not the other way around. Psychologist Jonathan Haidt introduced an elegant analogy of the rider and the elephant to visualize this. When the elephant (the limbic brain governed by emotion and instinct) decides to go somewhere, its rider (the rational, logical neocortex) has little choice but to go along.

Our thinking tends to rationalize decisions we have already made and things we have already done. When we say we are "going with our gut," we're just being sensible enough to give in to a decision-making process that works faster than we can think. But why does that matter?

It matters because we tend to try and influence what people *think* about brands. But what they think is unlikely to make much difference to whether they buy the brand. We need only care about how they *feel* about brands. That's difficult, of course, because we don't know the *reason* (neocortex) for our *feelings* (limbic). Hmmm.

What we do know is that feelings are governed by emotions, images, and ideas, and that they are all embedded in long-term memory. So, when we talk about mental availability, we shouldn't focus on the rational aspects of brands that can be sensibly considered at the point of purchase; we should focus on the emotional resonance of brands that drives our actions at the point of purchase.

As we consider the evolution of marketing from the broadcast era to the Attention Economy, that may be the most important shift we need to keep in mind: from the consideration of what people think about the brand to a focus on how they feel toward a brand; from the communication of facts to the imprinting of emotional associations.

A shift from the rational to the emotional. The factual to the conceptual. The controlled to the uncontrollable.

And to do that, we need to embed concepts, ideas, or "truths" about the brand into long-term memory (as distinct from embedding facts about the brand into short-term memory).

Defining the Brand

Before delving into the practicalities of finding the brand truth, we need to take an important detour and agree on some language around the brand.

Apologies if this seems terribly pedantic, but an unfortunate truth of any discussion about marketing or communications is that very often, people can use the same word and yet define it completely differently. The outcome is that two people can have a conversation using the same words without realizing that they are talking about two completely different things.

However, so much has been written about what brands are, and so many challenges have been made to every attempt at definition, that I don't want to go too deeply into a wormhole of brand theory. Rather, I'm just going to be declarative for the sake of clarity and precision. So, I'd like to offer definitions for three fundamental concepts: the brand, branding, and brand building.

One of my favorite definitions of the brand came from a British advertising man named Winston Fletcher, who described the brand as "the glittering haze." What was so appealing about it was the elegant precision of a very imprecise definition. It succeeded in describing what many practitioners recognized as a brand—a glittering, exciting constellation of thoughts, words, and images. And yet it said very little of practical use.

More recently, and more practically, Simon Sinek has drawn a great deal of attention to his idea of how great leaders inspire action—something he calls the golden circle. The golden circle is, in fact, three circles. In the center is a circle called "Why." One ring out from it is a circle called "How," and the outer ring is a circle called "What." He maintains that the world's great leaders communicate from the inside circle to the outside circle. They start with "Why." His view is that all organizations know "what" they do—the outer circle—(what they make, what services they provide); most organizations know "how" they do what they do—the middle circle—(their "uniqueness," their USP, their proprietary technologies, their IP); but few know "why" they do what they do—the inner circle. And those few are the ones that enjoy the greatest success. They implicitly understand their reason for being, their beliefs, their cause.

Once again, there have been many challenges to Sinek's thinking, but it does offer an elegantly simple definition of not just what makes inspirational leaders great, but what makes the brands they create great.

The brand is the "why." The beliefs. The truth. The best brands know their truth and that truth reflects what their audience believes about themselves; the worst brands do not. For great brands, the truth will exist before the brand name or the trademark does—sometimes long before. Those things can come later, and they can change and evolve. But the truth is a constant because, for many successful brands, the truth is embedded in the beliefs and values of the founder.

Nike is clearly one of the best-established, most evocative brands on the planet, but surprisingly, they were in business for many years before they were called Nike. In fact, they operated with a very clear sense of their brand truth for a full fourteen years before they changed their name. Between 1964 and 1978, they were Blue Ribbon Sports, first distributing Asics running shoes and then, in 1971, developing the first Nike-branded shoe. The shoe was so successful that they changed the name of the company in 1978. But even in those early years, their focus was consistent throughout. They focused on the competitor and the art of competition:

> The art of competing, I'd learned from track, was the art of forgetting, and I now reminded myself of that fact. You must forget your limits. You must forget your doubts, your pain, your past.

They focused on the transcendent power of sports:

> Sports give people a sense of having lived other lives, of taking part in other people's victories. And defeats. When sports are at their best, the spirit of the fan merges with the spirit of the athlete.

They focused on a belief in running and the runner:

Driving back to Portland I'd puzzle over my sudden success at selling. I'd been unable to sell encyclopedias, and I'd despised it to boot. I'd been slightly better at selling mutual funds, but I'd felt dead inside. So why was selling shoes so different? Because, I realized, it wasn't selling. I believed in running. I believed that if people got out and ran a few miles every day, the world would be a better place, and I believed these shoes were better to run in. People, sensing my belief, wanted some of that belief for themselves. Belief, I decided. Belief is irresistible."

And the evangelical zeal that underpinned everything they did:

Seek a calling. Even if you don't know what that means, seek it. If you're following your calling, the fatigue will be easier to bear, the disappointments will be fuel, the highs will be like nothing you've ever felt.[26]

The process of branding can also be thought of as trademarking. It is the creation of the name, the logo, the URL, the tagline, the hashtags, the design language (colors, typeface, photographic style), the verbal style (the tone of voice). It's what Byron Sharp refers to as the creation of distinctive brand assets: recognizable and reinforceable (and legally protectable) words, images, and sounds.

Nike's brand—its "truth"—was clear from inception. But its branding developed over time. The name was coined by Jeff Johnson, the first employee of BRS who was then running their East Coast factory (and the name was developed for the first shoe they developed—and only later applied to the whole company). The swoosh was designed in 1971—again for a shoe—by Carolyn Davidson, a graphic design student at Portland State University. The iconic "Just Do it" tagline wasn't written until 1988.

"Branding," trademarks, service marks, and distinctive brand assets can develop over time. Those assets can be modernized and sharpened. Trademarks like the Apple logo demonstrate a very elegant evolution over the last forty years: changing, modernizing, but still eminently memorable and identifiable. (Caveat emptor—the marketing world is littered with examples of brand refreshes that aren't memorable or identifiable, and they don't end well.) But while branding can evolve, the brand should be a constant.

Brand building is everything that's done once the brand is born. It is the dynamic, constant, ever-changing process of marketing and communication that follows the fixed development of the brand and its branding. It encompasses all aspects of the marketing and communications mix. It encompasses all the communication disciplines that the brand employs. It encompasses the media and the message.

Nike's first brand ad, which featured the famous headline "There is no finish line," ran in 1976. The first "Just Do It" campaign ran in 1988. Brand building is fluid, evolving. It recognizes cultural currents and swims with them.

So, with those definitions in mind, as we think about finding the brand's truth, it is the defining idea that we are searching for. (We'll tackle branding and brand building later.)

If we think about that defining idea in relation to the Nike example, it was captured in their focus on the transcendent power of sports, the belief in running and the runner, the evangelical zeal that underpinned everything they did.

Eventually, it was captured in a few very elegant words: Just Do It.

But long before that, the defining idea—the truth—was part of Nike the same way it was part of Phil Knight. He was the charismatic leader of his church, and his employees and customers worshipped alongside him. There was a central religiosity to the Nike brand, felt most fervently by the early apostles but felt nonetheless by people who attached themselves to the company as employees, partners, or customers.

That religiosity is something that is common among many great brands. The founding beliefs and values followed devotedly over time. And if you look at the elementary principles of religious life—like sociologist Émile Durkheim did—you'll notice many parallels between branding and religion.[27]

But that is too much of a wormhole, so here endeth that sermon.

The principle is important, though. The brand idea—its truth—isn't made up. It isn't invented. It isn't "spun." The brand truth needs to be either distilled or discovered.

Distillation and Discovery

For new brands, the process of finding their truth is one of distillation—consistently examining their reasons for being, why they do what they do, and boiling it down to an essence. A simple, memorable statement of purpose: *"Skincare first. Makeup second. Smile always." "Make America Great Again."*

For existing brands that don't have a well-articulated truth, the process is one of discovery. And that is important. The brand's truth isn't something that can be made up. It's something that exists in the history and culture of the brand, and it needs to be unearthed: *"Just Do It."*

Those examples of brand truth are also taglines for the brand. And there will be a lot of practitioners and academics who will argue that the tagline isn't a statement of purpose. Often, I would agree. But I'm also clear that perhaps the greatest skill of a talented copywriter is to boil very complex and nuanced concepts down into a few elegantly memorable words. And that's what happened in the examples above. When it does happen, you have found gold—a statement of the brand's truth that accurately (and powerfully) reflects why you do what you do. One that is understandable to consumers, so it becomes a distinctive brand asset. A statement that is, at the same time, an articulation of the brand's story and an invitation to participate in the story. When those elements combine, a certain kind of magic has been found.

Now, there is no suggestion here that this is an easy process. It can be brutally difficult, in fact. The relentless teasing of an idea, the worrying of the statement of purpose until it reveals itself cleanly and clearly, can be the most difficult job in the marketing business. Simplicity can be the hardest thing in the world to achieve. But it can also be the most effective once it is achieved. And it is possible to tell complete and engaging stories about a brand in very few words—as long as they are the right words.

(There is an unsubstantiated tale that Ernest Hemingway—a celebrated master of brevity and the *mot juste*, the perfect word for the perfect occasion—was once challenged to tell a story in six words. He wrote, "For sale. Baby shoes. Never worn.")

Importantly, whether you are distilling the brand's truth for a new brand or discovering it for an existing brand, the search for truth starts inside the company—not outside. The brand truth is a statement of purpose. It is not a "positioning statement." The process of positioning is one that finds the marketing "white space" for a product or brand to occupy. It is a concept indelibly linked to the salesmanship theories of advertising. It examines a category and determines where the brand's most attractive opportunity to compete lies. And, by definition, that attractively "unoccupied" space will change over time as competitors shift their priorities and continue to innovate and introduce new products and services.

Conversely, the truth of the brand—its "why"—shouldn't change. It operates at a level beyond (or before) competition. It is what Phil Knight described as "the calling," his "belief." And you can't change a calling. (Or maybe you can, but you probably shouldn't.)

So, a truth is different from a positioning. One is fixed, internally focused, and unchanging. The other is fluid, market (externally) focused, and fungible. This is an important distinction, if only because the idea of brand positioning is much better established than the idea of brand truth.

Brand positioning has been written about and discussed for years, ever since Al Ries wrote about the dawn of the "Positioning Era" in 1972. His wildly successful book *Positioning: The Battle for Your Mind*, written with Jack Trout, followed, and his own position as a marketing guru was cemented. (Interestingly, the foreword for *Positioning* is written by Philip Kotler, whose theory of brand loyalty, you may remember, was probably responsible for the work of Professor Andrew Ehrenberg being buried for so long.) Brand positioning is indeed a "battle for your mind."[28] It is a concept that focuses on finding uniqueness in a competitive category, which means it doesn't really fit with the ideas of Byron

Sharp and the Ehrenberg Bass Institute, who dismiss the need for uniqueness and reinforce the need for distinctiveness.

The idea of a brand's truth—its defining idea—has been written about less and is less well understood. Again, Simon Sinek's concept of "why" is helpful. A usefully concise view of it comes from Afdhel Aziz on Medium, who describes it as a "higher order reason for a brand to exist than just making a profit." (I think the higher-order reason for the brand to exist is the important part here—brands, even the most enlightened brands, seek to make a profit through their ventures.)

The process of finding that brand truth is very consistent, regardless of whether the brand is new, in which case the process is one of distillation, or the brand is in existence, in which case the process is one of discovery. Again, it starts from the inside. A simple set of questions—asked by a talented brand planner or strategist—is all that is required. Here are some examples:

- How did you begin? What is your origin story? What is your founding myth?
- What gets you up in the morning? What makes it exciting to keep going every day?
- What is your area of competency? What do you do well that other companies struggle with?
- What are you most proud of in your company or your culture? What do you brag about at dinner parties?
- Who do you serve? What do they come to you for help with?
- What do you most wish the world understood about you?

They seem simple. They are simple. But those simple questions, asked of the right people, in the right environment, with room to think, reflect, and answer without judgment or reproach, will yield the answers to what the brand stands for—its truth.

And then, with some judgment, a little luck, and the right talent, a wondrous alchemy may happen. Ideas distilled to their absolute essence, expressed in language wielded as a poet wields language, stop you in your tracks and make you think anew about something that's been staring you in your face. Emotions are elicited that completely bypass your neocortex and reach directly into your limbic system—your emotional brain—where thinking is turned off, feeling begins, and fame is created.

LIVE YOUR TRUTH

From Brand Identity to Brand Experience

Although Nike had a well-defined brand from inception—a clear sense of their truth, why they did what they did, they weren't branded Nike until fourteen years later. But in the Attention Economy, the brand is born fully dressed. The truth is clear, and the branding is complete from day one. Thinking back to the example of Glossier from earlier, the brand was fully formed ("In order for your makeup to look better, start with a skincare routine"). And the branding was evident immediately: the words, "Skincare first. Makeup second. Smile always," paired with millennial pink and images of smoky eyes and dewy skin. The brand and the branding walked in lockstep.

In the Attention Economy, information travels too fast, and questions or issues with a company or brand can find their way into the light at a speed that marketers have never had to contend with before. So, we don't have the luxury of separating the brand from the branding. As we're dressing the brand, we need to be very clear about what brand we are dressing.

One of the icons of broadcast-era business and marketing, Jack Welch of GE, coined the phrase "the naked truth" to describe the effect that the internet would have on a corporation's ability to maintain its privacy. And he rightly concluded that there was no such thing as corporate privacy anymore.

The naked truth is that if any company (particularly a very big one) is doing something naughty, someone will work it out. And once uncovered, they'll publish their findings as widely as they can. And once published, the credibility of the naughty company will diminish, making it harder for them to sell things. In the Attention Economy, people don't like closed doors; they like the open book. They don't want to be shut out. They want to be let in. People reward companies that operate with openness, liberty of information, and the power of community as central to the way they do business. Which means that a company's "truth," its belief, its values, its *brand*, needs to be clearly articulated from conception, and the brand needs to remain true to it.

Sharp has popularized the view that the key to creating mental availability is distinctiveness. Here, he's distinguishing between being distinctive and being unique, and that's a good distinction. (Although marketers have spent many decades searching for opportunities to stand alone in their categories, the reality is that we buy from a consideration set of broadly comparable products, and we don't think there's much difference between them—Coke tastes much like Pepsi.) He opined that it was more important to be distinctive within your category than it was to be unique within your category. All good so far. But—and this is a big but—Sharp defines distinctiveness as a "brand looking like itself," and the guidelines of "creating distinctive brand assets," "being consistent yet fresh," and "refreshing brand-linked memory structures" are approaches to "looking like yourself", and using that image—that picture—as a reminder that you're still around. But, as an approach to creating distinctiveness and mental availability in the Attention Economy, the naked truth is that it is an oversimplification.

Looking like yourself as a brand is much like looking like yourself as a person. It presents an image of you but doesn't define you. Steve Jobs was a brand and a person. He had a very well-branded uniform that he dressed in every day—blue jeans and a black sweater. His hair was distinctively buzzed, he maintained the same length of scruffy stubble, and he always wore the same wire-framed eyeglasses. He was quickly recognizable and, when compared to other CEOs of multibillion-dollar corporations, he was distinctive in his dress.

But while Shakespeare wrote in *Hamlet* that "the apparel oft proclaims the man," it may proclaim him, but it does not define him. Now we all know that, don't we? It would be superficial to judge a book by its cover. But we do it. There's no denying that the presentation of anything affects our impressions of it. This is the magical power of design. But we also know that to understand a person or a brand, we need to look beneath the cover. And we do that regularly, even if we do it subconsciously.

If Steve Jobs had walked into a party and started spinning plates on a stick, doing card tricks, and telling bawdy jokes while smoking a cigar, his friends would have wondered what was wrong with him. Perhaps they would go as far as to wonder if it was someone who looked like him and dressed like him, because it clearly didn't seem like him. We do the same with brands.

When brands do things, or say things, or act in certain ways, we judge them. That judgment is subconscious, but we judge them nonetheless. We decide whether those words or those actions felt right to us. If they don't, we reject them. We screen them out. We decide (way before we've processed it rationally) that they don't fit our view of the brand, and so, we ignore them. The principle of confirmation bias kicks in. We are presented every minute of every hour with information and entertainment from brands and people. It could be overwhelming, but we have a very good process for avoiding being overwhelmed, which is that if something doesn't fit into our belief systems—if it doesn't connect to a K-Line that we have already developed on a subject—we get rid of it. In brand terms, that action has been wasted. The money and effort spent on it have been wasted. No communication has taken place. It may have been sent, but it has not been received.

Any brand, but particularly a large international brand, says and does thousands of things every day. And every one of those things communicates something about the brand.

Those actions cannot be regulated alone by a style guide or a branding framework. The framework would be too big. The style guide would never be read. Those actions need to be *felt*. They need to feel right. And in order for them to feel right, literally thousands of people who shape the brand (from marketing and communications people to sales and service people, to product designers and supply-chain experts) need to know why they are doing what they are doing. They need to understand the truth of the brand and their role within it. And they need to stay faithful to it.

From Appearances to Actions

So, back to the idea of distinctiveness being created by brands looking like themselves. The elements that make a brand look like itself are brand assets like logos, colors, product design, packaging design, web U/X, symbols, taglines, and advertising mnemonics.

All those things are important. Sometimes, when executed artistically, they can become magically important. And it's very tempting to focus on these elements of branding as being central to the brand because they are controllable and manageable. They are legally defensible—you can trademark them and protect that trademark in a court of law. And they are measurable—your brand-tracking study will tell you whether they are memorable.

But, just like Steve Jobs's jeans and sweater, they don't define the brand. All those things are actions that the brand undertakes: a new design, an updated package. Again, all those things are important. But there is something that is much more important.

It's not enough to find your truth; you need to live your truth.

Branding is something we do; the brand is something we are. A strong brand results when an organization, big or small, has such a clear sense of self that every word it utters or act it enacts is consistent with that sense of self and reinforces the story the brand tells about itself—why it does what it does. That's not an easy thing to do, but it is centrally important.

Most important is that that doesn't happen just because it has a good logo. The good logo is something that comes later. As we saw, for some brands, it's something that comes much later. Nike operated under a different name for the first fourteen years of its operation. But its principles were consistent. Its operation was consistent. Its belief in the power of competition and the competitor was consistent. And that consistency in belief, values, and execution makes it a powerful brand. When there is a break between belief, values, and execution, the brand has a problem.

Take, for example, the fate of some of the world's most powerful brands over recent years: the Catholic church, the British monarchy, and the United States. Each of these institutions implicitly understands the power of the brand. The "logos" and symbolism of each are world-famous. Their use of color and imagery is consistent. Their pageantry is lauded. Their rituals are embraced. They have distinctive brand assets, and those assets are applied consistently.

But each of them has faltered in recent years because of a disconnect between our idea of them and their actions—their brand and their branding. There was a clear disconnect between the idea of Catholicism and abuse. There was a clear disconnect between the queen of England and the treatment of "the People's Princess." And there has been a clear disconnect between the idea of a *United* States and the partisan fervor of a divided nation.

The symbolism of these brands didn't change; neither did their logos, their signature colors, or their rituals. But our view of them, our belief in them, did change. And it changed because of a break between the idea of that brand and the way it acted.

The brand is the idea that guides us. It guides our actions— our hundreds or thousands (or millions, maybe) of actions every single day. *It stands to reason here that it's important to "know" what the brand's idea is. But remember: knowing is reason. It's the neocortex. It's short-term memory. And therein lies the rub.* If we are trying to govern what may be literally millions of actions that impact the brand every single day (think about the operation of McDonald's on a global basis for a second), then we just can't write a rulebook big enough to manage those actions. And if we could, no one would read it. And if someone read it, they wouldn't remember it.

So, it would be nice to think that we can know what the brand's idea is and that we can be true to it. But it's much more important that we "feel" what the brand is and, therefore, what is right and what is wrong for a brand. It's more important that we live that truth.

That sounds a bit fluffy, doesn't it? How can you expect to successfully manage a multibillion-dollar brand based on feelings? But that is the reality of what happens every single day.

For example, my company recently won an Agency of Record assignment with one of the world's largest multinational consumer goods companies. They own over one hundred brands. Many of them are billion-dollar brands in their own right.

Their onboarding process was world-class: clear and deep overviews of operating conditions, marketing operations, the brand, and its customers. One meeting was particularly good. It was for a brand that, on a cultural basis, is said to define the operations of the entire company—a family favorite in America and around the world for decades. The brand team was, subconsciously, dressed in pops of the brand color.

At the end of a brilliant presentation on the past, present, and future of the brand, the team leader gave us an honest and prescient assessment of the challenge we faced. In her words, "Coming up with ideas and activations that are right for the brand is going to be the hardest thing you do. It's what every agency struggles with. We have worked on the brand for years. And over time, you just *feel* what's right."

Now, this is a brilliantly well-established brand, with logos, colors, symbols, and codes that have been in the market for years. They have brand books and campaign guidelines that are well-written, thoughtfully executed, and thorough. And yet the successful execution of the brand depends on knowing when something feels right.

The implication is that to become popular, it's not enough to show up wearing the same clothes every day. It will help, but it's not going to get you invited to a lot of parties. What's more important is to have a very clear sense of who you are and to be true to that sense of self. The branding is important, yes. But the brand—the truth—is at least as important.

Now, clearly, it's helpful if that sense of who you are is likable and appealing to a broad range of people. But it's essential that you're not trying to be something you're not. And it's important that you're not saying things or acting in a certain way just because you think it will make you more popular. It has the opposite effect. It shows you to be untrustworthy, inconsistent, and inauthentic.

And authenticity has never been more important, which can be ably demonstrated by looking toward the rising sun.

Streetwear in Japan has become a big industry for the fashion-forward. In the late '70s, Japanese kids started to rebel against the restrictions and values that were being imposed on them by their parents and began to express their own values and belief systems through their choice of clothes. However, given that there had been no youth culture in Japan before that point—with its associated creatives and designers—the clothes that were used to express those values were imported: college-preppy and workwear styles from the US, casual-chic from Italy.

The dynamic had a profound business effect on traditional American apparel brands. Suddenly, there was a new, and sizable, international market for Levi's jeans, New Era caps, Carhartt jackets, and Red Wing boots. Importantly, though, the items that became popular weren't new styles made from updated, modern fabrics. They were the original pieces, made in American factories, from traditional fabrics and to traditional patterns or lasts. More important than the logo was the story behind the piece of clothing.

That story became easier to establish as the search functionality of the internet became more robust. And Japanese kids perused the stories of factories, fabrics, and styles with fetishistic zeal to find the brands—and the pieces from those brands—that were most authentic and had the best backstory.

Now, although this is only one example, and granted, it is an example of attention to detail and love of the story that comes from the country that invented the Bonsai tree, the principle of understanding the roots of a brand and the authenticity of its story is something that applies to all brands now. Does the beauty brand that claims to be "natural" use exclusively natural products? What does cage-free really mean? Is a carbon-neutral claim just a cheap way to deflect attention from climate-aggressive business practices?

These questions are being asked regularly of brands in the Attention Economy, particularly by younger, digitally native consumers. And the answers to them define how authentic a brand's story is. The naked truth is that there's no hiding. Brands need to do what's right—and what's right for them. They need to be true to their idea and their purpose. Otherwise, we'll turn away from them—even if they're wearing their best clothes.

The Need for Symbolism

The psychologist Paul Watzlawick wrote, "It is impossible not to communicate."

Everything we do says something about us. The decision to wear a suit and tie rather than jeans and a T-shirt to a business meeting says something about us. The minute we walk into the room, nonverbal communication has taken place between the wearer and the watcher. It suggests how we feel about the room and the seriousness of the meeting or the occasion. How we feel about the other people in the room. Are we deferring to them, or do we feel they should be deferring to us? Are we modern or traditional? Our clothes are a medium, and the clothes we wear are a message.

The same applies to brands. There is symbolism in everything. It is impossible not to communicate.

One of the things that most notably distinguishes the digitally native brands that grew up in the Attention Economy from their broadcast-era competitors is their understanding of how to use symbolism to their advantage.

Consider, for example, the difference between naming approaches to classic mattress brands like Simmons (named after its founder, Zalmon Simmons) or Tempur-Pedic (a healthcare-style mashup of words—temperature and orthopedic) and attention-economy brands named after sleepy ghosts (Casper) or traditional construction techniques (Tuft & Needle).

The latter name has been discussed often enough that the founders wrote the origin story on the company blog.

> Later, when JT and Daehee were brainstorming what they might name their new company, JT remembered his experience [of making a mattress under the tutelage of a master upholsterer] and wrote "tuft" and "needle" in the long list of words that resonated with them. They knew they wanted something original, nothing sounding old or tired like the industry they wanted to disrupt. Names that included "sleep" or "mattress" just wouldn't work. Their goal was to create a name, and a company, that was authentic, craftsman-like, original, timeless and modern.

All the principles the Tuft & Needle founders wrote about were intuitively followed but are beginning to become clearer as patterns for building attention-economy brands. In their words, they wanted a name that was "original and not tired," one that was "authentic, craftsman-like, timeless and modern." (And you can see the same thing happening across categories: athletic footwear called "Allbirds," gym wear called "Outdoor Voices," and even in the category that most of us would actively like to avoid talking about—insurance—we have an insurgent brand called "Lemonade" [because when life gives you lemons, make lemonade].)

In every instance, there's something notable in the name, something worthy of comment, question, or discussion. (And from a practical perspective, it makes it easier to trademark, secure a URL, and find hashtags that work.)

Again, this isn't an entirely new dynamic. Virgin is a brilliant attention-generating brand with a brilliantly provocative name. And that choice of name instantly gave it an advantage in talk-ability over its more pedestrian-sounding competitors—like the Universal Music Group, when it was a record company, or, later, British Airways. But it is a skill that has been honed by more recent attention-economy marketers, as has the skill of creating engaging logos.

The distinction between broadcast-era logo development and the trademarking of the Attention Economy is seen nowhere more clearly than in the financial services category.

Traditional brands follow traditional design cues: lots of blue and red, lots of boxes, and traditional typefaces for their word-marks. The more modern brands look instantly different—mod-ern, energetic, engaging. They look more innovative, and they look more approachable.

Now, just to be clear, I don't expect that there have ever been long conversations involving many thousands of people about the elegance of the cursive font in the logo for Lemonade insurance. I do, however, think that if a reporter is asked to write an overview of the insurance industry, it will immediately make their article more interesting if they include a reference to home and renters' insurance from Lemonade and health-care insurance from Oscar.

Making Design Conversational

Arguably even more fundamental than name and logo design is product design and packaging. And that, clearly, can be made conversational.

Thinking back to the story of Nike, the name and logo came fourteen years after the inception of the company. But Bill Bowerman (Knight's track coach at the University of Oregon) had been experimenting with running shoe soles—using a waffle iron in his garage—long before the name existed.

Physical design can define a brand and, without question, can create an enormous volume of conversation around it.

The success of Apple under the design stewardship of Jony Ive is a clear demonstration of this. Provocative, engaging, and youthful design became a hallmark of the Apple brand in its second life, after the return of Steve Jobs in the late '90s. And a string of product and technology successes bore witness to the magic of the partnership between Jobs and Ive and their joint commitment to the centrality of product design.

The first product they unveiled in that new era was the iMac, which Ive designed with a translucent plastic cover in an array of fruit-inspired colors. That alone generated a wealth of conversation about the brand and the business. With that singular statement, Apple was back. (It also inspired my favorite classified advertisement of all time: in the back of a computer magazine, surrounded by small square ads for various computers highlighting their "speeds and feeds," was a similarly small ad for the iMac with a headline that declared, "Now available in Blueberry.")

That kind of playful energy in product design is now seen consistently among the digitally native brands that grew up in the Attention Economy—from Casper's concept of the "bed in a box" to Away designing their affordably iconic luggage with a built-in phone charger.

But physical design isn't limited to the intrinsic design of a product. Brands can generate conversation for themselves by being creative with the extrinsic elements of the product—its packaging.

Apple has become justly famous for this too. One of the joys of purchasing Apple products is the unboxing—which is inevitably well thought through, elegant, and instructive—giving the buyer a sense of the energy the brand puts into every aspect of the customer experience.

But there are many other examples of how brands have used creative twists in their packaging to generate conversation.

In the run-up to the 2016 presidential election, for example, Budweiser changed the name on its can to "America," a move undertaken, in their words, "to inspire drinkers to celebrate America and Budweiser's shared values of freedom and authenticity." Regardless of whether it really was a celebration of Bud's values of freedom and authenticity, it created a firestorm of conversation around the brand and its marketing—1.6 billion impressions overall (equivalent to two Super Bowl ads).

Interestingly, in this example, it wasn't just the brand name that changed on the can. The words "King of Beers" were replaced with *E Pluribus Unum* ("out of many, one"). The beer's ingredients, which are usually found evocatively written at the top of the can, were replaced with the lyrics to "The Star-Spangled Banner." And yet, in testament to just how distinctive the brand asset of the Budweiser can is, at first blush, the America can looks identical to the classic version.

The can was designed by the British-based design firm Jones Knowles Ritchie, and they are no strangers to talkable packaging design. When they realized that 96 percent of all Domino's pizzas are bought in pairs, they took the opportunity to redesign the pizza boxes as actual dominoes, once again to much conversation and hullabaloo.

And if you wondered why your morning cup of Dunkin' seemed to taste just that little bit more delicious a few years ago, it may have been because they embraced the brand's vibrant pink-and-orange color scheme and their iconic bubble type to proclaim, on all their packaging, the myriad ways that America really "runs on Dunkin'." Once again, earning billions of impressions for the brand (over one billion of them in the first twenty-four hours after the rebrand).

Designing the Narrative

There is a very practical reason to think about designing the brand's narrative, which is that without the "controlled communication" of paid media campaigns, the brand's logo is not guaranteed to be seen.

It seems obvious, really. If a journalist writes a front-page article about the athletic performance benefits of eating Wheaties in the morning, they are unlikely to include the Wheaties logo. But the Wheaties article is an unquestionably important brand-building tool.

It will still be read by the people who subscribe to the *New York Times*. But more importantly, social media will act as a force multiplier for that readership as the social media icons under the digital article are clicked, and the content is shared. And the force will be multiplied once again when people read that article in their friends' social media feeds and "like" it, comment on it, or retweet it.

So how does Wheaties make sure that they are reinforcing their brand as people read, comment, and talk about the article?

Well, equally obviously, words are simple and effective brand identifiers. The name of the brand will always be used, and that is arguably its most important brand asset. (And we'll look later at what work can be done to make that asset more distinctive.) The brand's tagline will often be used as a descriptor. Imagine this, for example: "Wheaties has long promised to be the breakfast of champions, but this breakthrough study first published in the *New England Journal of Medicine* proves that there may be more to the claim." The brand is referenced in a way that could ignite the "K-Line" connections we have about the benefits of eating a fiber-rich breakfast cereal.

To shift from the hypothetical to the practical, we can go back to one of our case studies from the start of the book and examine Donald Trump's campaign for the GOP presidential candidacy.

To remind you, Trump was consistently outspent by practically everyone else on the ballot. Ted Cruz had spent more than double what Trump had on advertising. Jeb Bush had outspent him by 800 percent. But Trump was mirroring his competitors' dominance in paid media with his own dominance of earned media. And the overall volume of earned media dwarfed the paid media exposure.

Now, it won't take much to imagine this from an article in any national newspaper or a report from any national broadcast journalist: "The stadium was packed with MAGA-hat-wearing Trump supporters chanting, 'Build that wall!'" I made that up, but I'm almost sure I read it a million times. That simple sentence includes four distinctive brand assets.

The stadium rallies were a hallmark of the Trump campaign and his presidency. The words "stadium rallies" now immediately conjure up images of Trump. The MAGA hat itself was a visual asset—but the description of the red baseball cap with the words "Make America Great Again" as a MAGA hat made it immediately evocative. (You only need to hear or read those words for the image to appear in your mind.) The name Trump is a distinctive brand asset. The chant "Build that wall" once again immediately conjures images of Trump and his campaign. So here we have four very distinctive and evocative brand assets in one sentence. We have conjured up very clear images of the brand. And yet, we haven't seen anything that connects us to the brand.

On the flip side, I would challenge anyone to remember anything that connects them to the presidential nomination campaigns of Ted Cruz or Jeb Bush. Although they massively outspent Trump in paid media, their controlled messages and the visual brand assets they employed didn't stick.

To create a positive brand effect, though, all those words, those brand assets, must be singing from the same song sheet. All of them must be consistently true to the brand. Otherwise, we will reject them, and the opportunity for Wheaties to capitalize on a front-page article in the *New York Times* will be wasted.

We knew what Trump's truth was: America First, Make America Great Again, and his advisors' mantra, "Let Trump be Trump." He was unfailingly consistent in thought, word, and action. And the earned media he generated had a powerful brand effect as a result.

Designing the Experience

We've looked at a few examples of talkable experience design already. Virgin Airlines has done a particularly good job of it for years. From the "pinched from Virgin Atlantic" saltshakers to the Vivienne Westwood flight crew uniforms and the walk-up bar on the plane. But their commitment to talkable experiences extends beyond that.

Their airline lounge in Heathrow Airport has become justifiably famous, for example. Passengers can get their hair cut for free by Bumble and Bumble stylists before settling down for playfully delicious British meals—bacon butties for breakfast and fish and chips with mushy peas for dinner, before heading to the bar for cocktails and enjoying a game of pool or a movie. Everything about the experience in the Virgin Atlantic lounge brings to life the personality of the Virgin brand, an approach that was employed to great effect by some of the earliest attention-economy marketers.

The approach was pioneered by brands like Nike and Apple, who created NikeTown and the Apple Store, respectively. Interestingly, both of those experiences were designed by the same team at a small design firm in San Francisco called Eight Inc. And the principles that underpinned the development of both concepts are clear in the words of the co-founder of the firm, Tim Kobe, in a *Fast Company* article about the design process.

> What ultimately made the design of the Apple stores distinctive (and distinguished) was the way in which the design team, as Kobe explains, led with key values; the driving principles of Apple mobilized them. Those principles together served as the entry point into a project filled with uncertainty, igniting a making process that carried forward into the design. "When you think about what made Apple special," Kobe reflects, "it was about [making] technology accessible to people other than engineers. That's what the mouse did— it wasn't keystrokes and backstrokes and writing code. It was about making technology human.[29]

And with its open spaces and community display tables, the PDA checkout process and the Genius Bar, the Apple Store made technology as human and accessible as Apple products did—it reflected the truth of the Apple brand (something that couldn't be accomplished in retail locations that Apple didn't control). All of which led Steve Jobs to state, "The store is our best product yet!"

The same approach to physical retail as a manifestation of the brand experience is something that is coming to define the attention-economy marketer (Tesla decided to put their "dealerships" in high-end shopping malls, for example). But what distinguishes the best practitioners is their ability not just to create a brand experience, to tell their truth, but to get it talked about.

Glossier, for example, has defined its brand in large part through the experience of being in the stores. For them, e-commerce is where people buy products, and physical retail is where they experience the brand. But beyond experiencing the brand, Glossier wants its fans to talk about it. And the experience of chatting with the millennial-pink-jumpsuit-clad "editors," taking pictures next to the human-sized tubes of Boy Brow, and hanging out and meeting new beauty fans like them is all designed to earn attention and get people talking about the brand.

> If they're not taking pictures in your store then they're not talking about you. So, make them talk about you.

Clearly, though, talkable brand experiences don't just exist in the physical realm. Building delightfully surprising moments into UX design can make the brand's digital experience worth talking about too.

Gamification is one of the approaches that's being used to that end, tapping into our essentially competitive nature to make all manner of experiences more enjoyable and more talkable. Headspace made meditation more accessible by gamifying their digital experience, for example. And Duolingo gamified their app to make learning a new language more fun (and they earned over 1.3 million reviews on the App Store in return). They also amassed two million followers on TikTok by being playful with a life-size mascot modeled on their green owl logo (a particularly distinctive brand asset). Doing things that, in the words of their social media manager Zaria Parvez, are:

> Absolutely unhinged. Like our content is a lot of Dua Lipa fangirling, funny memes that probably

have like five too many layers of the internet on
it, just having a good time honestly, and doing
things you wouldn't expect a language-learning
app to do.[30]

All of it is youthful, energetic, engaging, and provocatively
stupid fun that people want to share and talk about.

But while UX and app design can create a more talkable
brand experience in a digital environment, the communication
discipline that may contribute most to talkable engagement in
digital is content marketing.

Designing Content

The one-two punch of performance media combined with
engaging, talkable content is arguably one of the most practical
and powerful tools in the workshop of the attention-economy
marketer.

Practical because, as we've discussed at length, all brands
now are obliged to divert significant proportions of their marketing funds toward performance-oriented, sales-driving digital
media. So it is practical—probably to the point of essential—that
attention-economy marketers find ways to build long-term
salience into their brands with that performance-oriented budget. But it can be powerful, too, when brands add engaging content to their sales outreach.

The cycling apparel brand Rapha is a particularly good
example of this. The brand was launched in 2004 and has since
grown to exert an outsized cultural force on the world of cycling.
They are in every way an attention-economy marketer, and every
aspect of their brand has a subtle but inherent talkability to it.

They were named after a slightly obscure European cycling team from the '60s, which immediately hints at the obsessive nature of the brand. As a consumer, you get the sense that they love the sport to the point of fetishization. And indeed, their stated purpose is to "Make cycling the most popular sport of the world," and the first value they list—which they expect future employees to live by—is to "love the sport [and make it part of your life]."

The thing that got Rapha talked about first was their product design. In a dramatically understated departure from the cycling apparel norms of the time, they rejected garish graphics and loud colors and designed their shorts and jerseys with a single white band and "hidden" flashes of pink as the only graphic elements against monotone fabrics. In another departure from the norm, they employed modern versions of traditional performance fabrics, like merino wool for jerseys and leather for gloves. And their pricing was notably high, giving the brand an aura of luxury. The design was instantly iconic and was talked about and debated relentlessly in cycling circles.

But the commitment to living the sport didn't stop at product design. It carried through to everything the brand does.

In marketing terms, Rapha is something of an anomaly. In some respects, their playbook is similar to other digitally native brands. They sell almost entirely through e-commerce, but they operate twenty or so Clubhouses around the world, which act as physical retail locations but, maybe more importantly, offer customers an immersive experience of the brand (with bike races on TV, espresso served at the bar, and high-end bikes for rent). But unlike many digital marketers, they are entirely unintrusive in their approach.

If you Google "cycling apparel," for example, there is no Google ad at the top of the page for Rapha. But their organic search position is high—because a lot of people seek out the brand. They do, however, make regular use of one of their owned-media assets, which is their email list.

Rapha is a very active email marketer, and email marketing is a bedrock tool of performance marketing. But what distinguishes them from other email marketers is that you actively look forward to receiving their emails because the content is inevitably beautiful, engaging, and true to the sport. In some ways, they act more like documentarians than marketers. Their photography and video content always has a real sense of verisimilitude (never thought I'd get that word into a passage about content marketing). Their content is at once familiar and aspirational—you recognize the feelings of their riders through their expressions, you recognize the environments, the roads, and the trails they are riding, and you immediately want to be riding with them.

As you click through to the website, the heart of the owned-media environment (as I invariably do), the experience is consistent—unobtrusive and engaging. Even their site navigation is telling in its inviting nature. The first two buttons on the navigation bar are for the men's and women's stores. The third is for the club, and the fourth is for their "stories."

The club has become central to the Rapha experience and is a powerful owned medium. Somewhere around fifteen thousand people pay seventy dollars per year for membership into the Rapha Club, which buys you access to exclusive club kit, discounts on bike rental and coffee at the Clubhouses, and invitations to cycling club events (like weekly group rides or presentations from cycling luminaries). The unwritten benefit is that it buys you access to a group of like-minded people in major cities around the world.

The club is an engaging and talkable aspect of the Rapha brand. The club kit is a very distinctive brand asset (with pink as the dominant accent color against black fabrics). And the club events are popular and well attended. But Rapha stories sit even closer to the heart of the brand.

The stories range from the educational (product guides, guides to riding in winter, and overviews of professional teams, for example) to the truly engaging.

One example is the "Alt Tour," where they documented Lachlan Morton (an Australian professional rider with the EF team) attempting to ride the full Tour de France route entirely self-supported and get to Paris before the Peloton. In classic Rapha fashion, the attempt was bold and inspirational, and the film of the challenge was a great short-form documentary. (Spoiler alert: after riding 5,510 km over eighteen days, he made it to the finish line five days before the Tour riders and raised £500,000 for World Bicycle Relief in the process.)

It's hard to accurately gauge the media impact of the effort because so many of the video views were on Rapha's site. But there were 250,000 views of the film on the Rapha Films YouTube channel, another 65,000 on Team EF's channel, and 30,000 on BikeRadar's channel. And there are a full eight pages of video-search results on Google on top of that. The effort was also reported on by the BBC, NBC, all the global cycling press, and a raft of other lifestyle and news outlets. And that is just one of hundreds of stories on the Rapha site. Like any of the best attention-economy marketers, they recognize that they are a media owner and that if they use their owned media widely, they can build their brand effectively without having to pay other media owners to use theirs.

GET PEOPLE TALKING

From Advertising to Publicizing

As we've seen, the issue with much of the broadcast-era brand building is its reliance on paid media advertising to get noticed and reach prospective buyers (along with the broadcast-era assumptions that underpin it).

That reliance on paid media—and the marketing assumptions it created—was fine when we could rely upon controlled messages being consumed by a receptive audience. But for many reasons—either because we can't afford to, because we can't reach an audience that is big enough, or because our budgets are being diverted to things we didn't used to have to pay for—we can't rely on paid media to build our brands anymore. And if we continue to do so, we will continue to see a decline in marketing effectiveness. But there is a demonstrably effective (and theoretically supported) alternative.

The central issue that marketers are dealing with in the Attention Economy is that they can't afford to pay to optimize the bottom of their sales funnel and the top of their sales funnel at the same time. The costs to optimize the bottom of the funnel are increasing, while the costs to buy large audiences for the top of the funnel are becoming progressively less affordable—more money for smaller audiences.

But what we've seen in our examination of the social, cultural, and commercial success stories that have emerged from the Attention Economy is that they have all done a masterful job of earning an audience that, at one time, they would have paid for. They approach their marketing with a different mentality from the broadcast-era marketers who went before them. They think about earning attention rather than trying to buy it. That mindset has changed the way progressive companies are building their brands, as well as the way progressive entertainers and media owners are creating content and building audiences.

Take the late-night talk shows in the US, for example. One of the staples of the media diet for decades, the late shows seemed to be losing their relevance as a new generation of hosts took over the reins. James Corden seemed to have a particularly difficult task: an essentially unknown (in the US) British anchor who was brought in to host the 12:30 a.m. *Late Late Show* in 2015.

Corden hitched his wagon to the belief that his popularity would be best gauged by looking at YouTube views of segments rather than the traditional measure of audience ratings for the show. His belief was that ratings were essentially a measure of who was awake at that time, but YouTube views were a measure of what people enjoyed and found entertaining.

And indeed, although the ratings for the *Late Late Show* weren't particularly inspiring, with an average of 1.3 million people tuning in, Corden remained under contract until he returned to London with his family in 2023. The secret lay in his nineteen million YouTube subscribers, many of them tuning in to that non-linear platform to watch his famous "Carpool Karaoke" performances (one of which, featuring Adele, has been viewed 196 million times).

Ratings are the international currency of the broadcast-era marketer. It is how they value and buy their audiences. But as we've seen, even when those marketers can afford to buy enough ratings to reach sufficient portions of their audiences (and in many categories—insurance, pharmaceuticals, and automotive, for example—they still can), those audiences often don't want to be bought and will skip the advertising targeted toward them.

So intuitive Attention-Economy marketers think less about delivering controlled messages to captive audiences through paid media. Instead, they look to instigate uncontrollable ideas to broad audiences through earned media.

While broadcast-era marketers assume that their audience is captive and receptive, Attention-Economy marketers assume that an audience is multitasking on multiple platforms and isn't paying much attention.

Where broadcast-era marketers assume a one-way communication between brand and consumer, Attention-Economy marketers hope for a two-way conversation. (I use the word "conversation" broadly.)

Where broadcast-era marketers assume that their message will be "received and understood," Attention-Economy marketers hope that it will be received and acted upon—whether that action is a like, a share, a retweet, or a comment.

Attention-Economy marketers assume that the consumer of the media or the message is an active participant. They are not passively waiting to be entertained or enlightened by content; instead, they are actively waiting to add to it and become part of the story.

The central goal of Attention-Economy marketers is to engage the audience and bring them along for the ride—not just passively entertain them, but to have fun with them.

Importantly, marketing activities that are created with Attention-Economy marketing principles can always be extended into traditional broadcast (paid media) environments. There is a saying we use regularly in my own agency: if an idea is good enough to be liked on Facebook, shared on YouTube, or written about in the *Huffington Post*, it will always work in paid media. The opposite, however, is not the case.

But this does raise a central question—and perhaps, in the minds of broadcast-era marketers, it will raise a central concern. Because we have successfully applied the principles of broadcast-era marketing for much of the last seventy years, and many great and enduring brands have been built in that time, the muscle memory for any marketer who began developing their professional chops any time before 2010 or so will be to apply the principles of broadcast-era marketer to building brands.

So how can we be sure that Attention-Economy marketing principles can build a successful, enduring brand? We know that they can build cultural successes. We know that they can make individuals famous. But how do we know that we can use those principles to create anything other than spectacle and notoriety? Can we create the next Coca-Cola by building popularity through owned, earned, and shared media? It's not an easy question to answer.

Media attribution has been the holy grail of marketing since before there was a holy grail. Sophisticated marketers and sophisticated research companies have tried to develop sophisticated attribution models that can accurately determine which aspects of their marketing and communications mix are contributing to their sales success (or failure). But the models are notoriously flawed.

A primary flaw is that the biggest marketing effects are consistently attributed to the biggest media platforms, regardless of whether those platforms have actually been employed. TV advertising campaigns are regularly credited with brand-building and sales success, even when there has been no TV advertising campaign. (When we don't know, we tend to assume.)

Another flaw of attribution models that's more pertinent to the discussion here is that they have no way of capturing the effect of earned media. There's no measure of the impact of a segment on *The Today Show*, an article in *Forbes*, a glowing review from a satisfied user, or the widespread sharing of a piece of content.

Although it was allegedly uttered well over one hundred years ago, the famous maxim from William Hesketh Lever—"I know that half the money I spend on advertising is wasted. My only problem is that I don't know which half"—is likely still true. (Or was it John Wanamaker who said, "Half the money I spend on advertising is wasted; the trouble is, I don't know which half"? Debate.)

In many ways, the lack of clear attribution from traditional media may be what drove so many marketers toward digital media, where "last-click" attribution can be measured accurately, even if it doesn't really tell you anything. So, in the absence of a clear method for measuring the effect of paid or earned media, how do we know that brands can earn popularity?

We can point out a few things that support the argument. One, straight from the mountaintop, is that the Ehrenberg Bass Institute—and indeed the great Andrew Ehrenberg himself—wrote a thorough yet rarely spoken-of paper that determined that the primary role of brand advertising was creative publicity—and that creative publicity could be achieved by any number of means: advertising, yes, but also PR, word of mouth, and sponsorships, for example. Second, that theme has been developed recently in two consecutive books from the brilliant Paul Feldwick, who chronicles the theories of advertising and brand building over the last century and suggests that the primary role of paid-media advertising is to create fame, in the same way that showmen like P. T. Barnum would generate fame.

From Persuasion to Publicity

The Ehrenberg-Bass Institute has been publishing a series of papers on marketing science for its "corporate sponsors" for the last couple of decades. While he was still alive, Andrew Ehrenberg regularly contributed to them. In 2002, he, along with his colleagues Neil Barnard, Rachel Kennedy, and Helen Bloom, wrote paper number thirteen, titled, "Brand Advertising as Creative Publicity."[31] If you can get hold of it, it's worth a read. To boil it down, the central thesis is that while there are many views on the role of brand advertising, most of them come down to the idea that it is designed to sell by persuading consumers of an important differentiating element of a brand. Yet they conclude that persuasion is not how advertising works.

Now, for most people who work in advertising or marketing, the perceived importance of persuasion is very familiar. The Ogilvy agency, for example, anchors their brand with the words, "We sell or else." The Ted Bates agency—and, specifically, their chairman, Rosser Reeves—invented the idea of the unique selling proposition, which still forms the center of many marketing and creative brief templates. The famous marketing professor Ted Levitt said,

"Differentiation is one of the most important strategic and tactical activities in which companies must constantly engage." But Ehrenberg and colleagues began to challenge that view.

> Our contrary thesis is that advertising and selling do not depend on consumers seeing the brand as different, but upon the brand being seen at all.

This idea that the brand does not have to be seen as different (and that it is enough that the brand is seen at all) is an important shift in marketing thinking. The truth is that persuasion, through the establishment of uniqueness and differentiation, requires the use of controlled messages—primarily advertisements in mass media. Because points of uniqueness are rarely interesting enough to generate conversation or commentary on their own. (You'd be hard-pressed to find a headline in the *New York Times* that declares that "CHIPS AHOY COOKIES NOW HAVE 10% MORE CHOCOLATE.") It's just not interesting.

But when the team at the Ehrenberg Bass Institute began to dissect, analyze, and test different advertisements for their effectiveness, they found that:

> When we deconstructed and tested advertising messages…they were often seen as only providing "talking-points"—ways of saying something about the brand and creatively publicizing it—and not "selling points", seen as differentiating the brands.

Further, those advertisements sought to *show the brand in some creatively memorable, yet often fairly meaningless way.*

That doesn't require a controlled message. Something creatively memorable often leads to a piece of entertainment in its own right and, therefore, something worthy of being talked about, shared, written about, or commented upon.

So, the institute drew a line in the sand: from brand advertising as persuasion to brand advertising as publicity. They went on to conclude that the publicity effect of brand advertising worked even for established brands in highly competitive categories because the key role of advertising (or branded communication more broadly) was not to persuade or convince consumers of something but rather to make them feel something at all.

> Publicity often does not seem to be trying to persuade consumers to change what they feel about the brand. It mostly only seeks to have consumers feel, think, and remember something about the brand at all.

And in doing so, this publicity could help create or build salience for the brand, which is a key concept in the lexicon of Byron Sharp and the Ehrenberg-Bass Institute, who define salience as *the presence and richness of memory traces which result in the brand coming to mind in relevant choice situations.*[32]

Salience is more than just awareness. It is the richness of "memory traces"—the joining up of neurological dots to create long-term memories of, and feelings toward, a brand. That, in aggregate, makes a brand feel bigger in the mind's eye. And they were clear that it was publicity, rather than persuasion, that would build that salience.

Publicity can help to maintain the number of people to whom the brand is broadly "Salient", the term we are using for the brand coming to mind, being familiar, safe and satisficing (i.e. being "good enough").

And further, that publicity could be created through any number of activities, including brand advertising, but in other ways too:

Salience can develop through advertising as publicity, PR, word-of-mouth, retail display, sponsorship, and especially, through previous brand usage.

And this is important. Salience can be built through any number of different communications activities. Brand advertising, yes. But also, PR and word of mouth, sponsorships, and retail displays. And there are many more ways to generate publicity and salience today than there were in 2002: content marketing, influencer activations, organic social media, community management, product integration, experiential marketing, and on and on. Some are new disciplines; some are reimaginings of disciplines that have been around in different forms for many years. But many of these could be grouped under the definition of earned-media disciplines (as opposed to paid disciplines of advertising and CRM, for example).

The implication here is clear: the brands that have established themselves as household names in the lives of people around the world—Coca-Cola, Clorox, Persil—have built their brands with a broadcast-era state of mind and broadcast-era reliance on paid media, particularly TV commercials. But while they may have assumed that their advertising worked because of its carefully and thoughtfully constructed persuasive messaging, it worked by generating publicity that led to rich memory traces in the consumer's mind. And, importantly, that publicity could have been created through any number of mediums or communications disciplines. It didn't rely upon a controlled message—that was unimportant in their analysis—and therefore, it didn't rely upon controlled (paid) media.

Fanning the Fame

Paul Feldwick is a celebrated thinker on brands and the author of two excellent books on the role of advertising in a historical context. In the first, *The Anatomy of Humbug*,[33] he set out to detail six dominant theories of how advertising works, which he listed as follows:

1. Advertising as Salesmanship
2. Advertising as Seduction
3. Advertising as Salience
4. Advertising as Social Connection
5. Advertising as Spin
6. Advertising as Showbiz

It's a fascinating read—not least because no one had thought to do it before. But what makes it most interesting is the realization that the theories of advertising effectiveness that govern the investment and execution of $705 billion globally[34] are largely based on anecdote and guesswork.

We all carry one or more of these theories in our heads as we do our jobs every day. But I would imagine that few of us take the time to stop and wonder where the theory we apply came from, and why we believe it or accept it. The reality is that many have been advanced and articulated by practitioners who wanted to sell more of what they did—whether that was Claude C. Hopkins[35] arguing that advertising could be applied according to scientific principles, Edward Bernays[36] declaring that cleverly applied public relations could shape and crystallize public opinion, or Rosser Reeves[37] stating that all advertising should be based on a unique selling proposition. These theories were, in large part, advertisements for the type of work the author did. Yet, impressively, they have passed the test of time and become—some more than others—unquestioned aspects of the marketing lexicon.

The ones that have embedded themselves most firmly are the first two families of thought: advertising as salesmanship—the persuasive view of advertising that Ehrenberg and his colleagues argued against—and advertising as seduction. (The first being better established than the second.)

The first, advertising as salesmanship, is likely the one most people are familiar with. Anyone who has uttered or written the words "unique selling proposition," "reasons to believe," "prospect," or "conversion" is applying salesmanship theories of advertising (or marketing) to their work. Whether consciously or unconsciously, they are working to the principle that advertising is a mainly rational process of persuading people to change their behavior. And that persuasion depends on a well-supported argument for why a given brand is better, more efficient, faster, or cheaper.

The second, seduction, is probably less well understood but, I would imagine, equally often applied. Anyone who has uttered or written the words "consumer insight" is applying the Motivational Research principles of Ernest Dichter to their work. And again, either consciously or unconsciously, they are rejecting the idea that advertising is a rational process of persuasion and conversion and instead seeing it as a process of shaping and reinforcing the existing attitudes people hold toward a brand. This body of theory was well articulated by Pierre Martineau in his book *Motivation in Advertising*, of whom Feldwick writes:

> Martineau stresses, again and again, how advertising uses visual symbolism and connotative language to create emotional associations. Such associations relate to the deeper emotional motivations of the consumer. "People… are changeable, suggestible, highly non-rational, motivated far more by emotion and habit and unconscious causes than by reason and logic."

Interestingly, Martineau's very "modern" views of the role of advertising—which wouldn't feel out of place in any brand planning department in the US—were written in 1957. And, interestingly too, over time, the area of motivational research has been largely forgotten as a body of theory and co-opted into a slightly uncomfortable mash-up with the salesmanship principles of advertising to create what Feldwick describes as "the benign conspiracy" that governs most advertising development today.

The benign conspiracy is a dualistic view of how advertising works (and an unsatisfying landing place for most practitioners). It creates a feeling that something doesn't quite add up, that something doesn't quite jive with what happens in real life. Yet most strategy tools and processes in most marketing departments and agencies will try and reconcile the competing views of salesmanship and seduction by examining consumer insights and brand truths (seduction) and connecting them to propositions and reasons to believe (salesmanship). Motivation and persuasion, living not quite in harmony.

But harmonious or not, those first two bodies of theory about how advertising works drive the creation and development of most advertising today. In turn, they underpin many of the assumptions that broadcast-era marketing is based upon—sometimes following one theory in isolation (compare the persuasive advertising for the Flex Shield family of products with the seductive advertising for the Nike family of products, for example). But, very often, by using a mashed-up combination of both theories (think about the advertising for most detergent brands, for example).

But those two theories have one thing in common: they start with a one-to-one view of the advertising process. The implicit belief is that advertising is a one-to-one communication between the brand and the consumer. And that belief requires that the process begin with a psychological understanding of the individual, making theories one and two different from theories three through six. That is, they start with the individual instead of the group.

It's worth noticing here that virtually all the discourses of both rational persuasion and subconscious seduction tend to conceptualize the advertising process as a one-to-one communication between brand and individual consumer—a conceptualization that carries through to most conventional ad-testing techniques. However, it may be very important to consider that the effects of advertising are, to a significant extent, social. Preference for a brand will be influenced by seeing others use it, by the conversations we share about it, or merely by the perception that a brand is popular with others.

The other four theories have significant overlaps between them. (And in some ways, you can think of them as another two groups of two.)

Next come the theories of Salience and Social. Salience comes from the fame or "creative publicity" view of advertising advanced by Andrew Ehrenberg, which we reviewed already. Central to that theory is the idea of "the meaningless distinctive": brands don't need to be different—or to persuade people of the important differences they do enjoy—they need only to be distinctive and memorable. Social, meanwhile, is the least well-formed of the six theories but recognizes the social, interrelational importance of communications: often we will do what we see others around us doing, and often we will like what we see others around us liking.

Spin and Showmanship, in many ways, are two sides of a very similar coin. Spin is based on the principles of shaping public opinion that were advanced by Edward Bernays, while Showmanship references the "Din, Tinsel, and Rockets" of P. T. Barnum's successful approach to creating fame and excitement. Importantly, Feldwick recognizes that although the ideas of spin and showmanship have been disregarded by many marketers and communicators over the years—probably because they didn't seem "science-y" enough to warrant serious consideration by serious professionals—they do, in fact, recognize a fundamental truth about how our beliefs and behaviors are influenced.

> So, PR from the 1920s on knew all the tricks of advertising and had fewer hang-ups about practicing them. But fundamental to it all, I think, was a bigger notion: that public opinion, culture, the world of meanings that we share, is not

absolute but always there to be influenced—and
that if you don't influence it yourself, others will.

Although they may not seem science-y enough to warrant
serious consideration, the reality is that the godfather of marketing science—Professor Andrew Ehrenberg—supported the
notion that creative publicity (Spin and Showmanship) was what
most brand advertising should seek to achieve.

One of the most distinctive (differentiating, even) aspects of
The Anatomy of Humbug is that Mr. Feldwick is careful, sensible,
and experienced enough not to be dogmatic in stating that one
theory of advertising is more robust than the others. He regularly
argues that there are times and places where each of them may
be the most appropriate to apply. However, he does begin to lean
toward the notion that fame and popularity may be the most
important objectives of advertising and communication.

> All of this evidence suggests that simply being
> famous, appearing to be ubiquitous and popular,
> are in themselves important factors in building
> brands—and that this may be a major function
> of advertising.

That is something he develops further in *Why Does the Pedlar
Sing?*[38] The book, in a nutshell, is a discourse on why advertising needs to embrace popular culture to achieve "widespread
and lasting fame" for brands. It argues that the goal for creative
people is "to produce advertising that is popular, distinctive
and famous." And it recognizes that "creativity is the artistry we
need in order to achieve popularity and fame for the brands we
advertise."

Although Paul Feldwick is very firmly an advertising man and, throughout both books, references theories and approaches to advertising, I would suggest that, particularly for the theories of Salience, Social, Spin, and Showmanship, the word "publicity" could be substituted for the word "advertising"—and that in doing so, the books have wider application and relevance than they do otherwise. Indeed, Feldwick does reference the fact that the theories he outlines apply beyond the confines of the advertising discipline or the world of paid media.

> These various implicit models, theories, or belief systems about advertising—Salesmanship, Seduction, Showmanship, and so on—exist independently of any particular medium and of any particular time.

And, with that, we have some of the most respected writers and commentators in advertising, marketing, and brand building lining up behind a view that stands in contrast to the rational, one-to-one theories that make up much of current marketing practice.

On one hand, Andrew Ehrenberg argues that the role of advertising is, in fact, creative publicity that generates salience (*the presence and richness of memory traces which result in the brand coming to mind in relevant choice situations*) and that salience can develop through any number of communication disciplines, *through advertising as publicity, PR, word-of-mouth, retail display, sponsorship, and especially, through previous brand usage.*

On the other hand, we have Paul Feldwick arguing that being famous, ubiquitous, and popular is the goal for brands and that it can best be achieved by, in his words, advertising, and in mine, publicity, that is, in turn, "popular, distinctive and famous." He illustrates his point with examples stretching from David Beckham's sarong to the winged Lion of Venice, which clearly *exist independently of any particular medium.*

These giants of marketing, advertising, and communications thinking are collectively advancing a view that brands are built through a form of creative publicity that creates rich memory traces in the mind of the consumer. And that the process relies not on a one-to-one understanding of the individual but on a broader, social understanding of the group. None of this relies upon paid media but does rely upon earning the attention and interest of the public.

Don't Break News, Make News

Interestingly, this isn't an entirely modern phenomenon.

Modern, digitally native brands offer a useful case study in using spin, showmanship, and publicity to make their brands famous, earning attention rather than paying for it. In the media environment they launched in, there wasn't a demonstrated need to build the brand through traditional advertising. Many of their peers and competitors were doing quite well without it. But it's important to remember that many successful companies that grew up in the primetime of broadcast-era marketing also managed to succeed without relying on paid media to build their brands.

Virgin Atlantic, for example, was a notable David to the Goliath of British Airways when it launched a competing transatlantic route in 1984. Richard Branson employed all his skills to earn attention for the job of making his airline aspirational and famous. Everything about the experience was designed to make the journey as enjoyable as the destination, and every aspect of the marketing was designed to be provocative, inviting, and to get people talking.

Of course, we take the name for granted now, but in a category dominated by "flag-carrying" airlines that were named for their home country—British Airways, American Airlines, Singapore Airlines, and so on—the name Virgin was as provocative as could be. Add in the anarchic script of the logo design, and it was a slap in the face to the staid and predictable airline industry. Without doing anything, the name itself invited its passengers to have fun and join the party. And everything that followed reinforced the feeling.

The flight crew uniforms were designed by Vivienne Westwood, the punk couturier who made her name dressing the Sex Pistols (who, perhaps not coincidentally, were signed to Virgin Records).

In one of the simplest and most elegant pieces of talkable design ever, the iconic salt and pepper shakers, which were designed in the form of childlike, bubble airplanes, were stamped on their base "pinched from Virgin Atlantic"—daring passengers to steal the silverware. And Branson himself contributed gleefully to the fun. Rappelling down the sides of buildings, parachuting into launch events, riding jet skis on the lake of the Bellagio Hotel in Las Vegas, Branson always had an eye for the spectacle and an ear for the headline.

And Branson was just one of many business leaders who fanned the flames of their brand's popularity. Ray Kroc from McDonald's, Howard Schultz from Starbucks, and, more recently, John Legere—the "Un-carrier" CEO of the "Un-carrier" telecoms company T-Mobile—the list goes on and on. Each of them unceasingly committed to their "truth"—the central principles that governed their actions—and, at the same time, energetically focused on doing things that got people talking.

But going back further, many of the playbook plays in the new media environment harken back to the days before the broadcast media environment existed.

In fact, the roots of this type of energetic and participative brand building can be traced as far back as the 1920s—and, specifically, to a chap called Edward Bernays, who, in the later part of his life, came to be known as the father of modern public relations.

Bernays was born in Vienna in 1891, and in 1893, he moved with his family to New York. He graduated from Cornell University in 1912, and his first job was as a journalist, which led him to join the Committee on Public Information during the First World War. This was an independent group, funded by the government, to build support for the war effort both at home and abroad.

He referred to his work with the CPI as "psychological warfare"—a sinister-sounding practice that used an understanding of mass psychology to shape public opinion.

The understanding of mass psychology wasn't new to Bernays. He was, notably, the nephew of Sigmund Freud—also Austrian, also from Vienna. And Freud's principles of psychology and neurology were a constant in his thinking. Bernays, and Freud before him, recognized group psychology as distinct from individual psychology. As Freud wrote: *A group is extraordinarily credulous and open to influence; it has no critical faculty.*[39]

This sentiment grounded the work and writing of Bernays. In 1923, he spoke to the mind of the group in saying: *The crowd does not mean merely a physical aggregation of a number of persons... the crowd is rather a state of mind.*[40]

And later, he went further to suggest: *The group has mental characteristics distinct from those of the individual, and is motivated by impulses and emotions which cannot be explained on the basis of what we know of individual psychology.*[41]

At the end of the war, Bernays realized he could apply his principles of psychological warfare to the task of molding public opinion in peacetime. To promote that idea, he published *Crystallizing Public Opinion* in 1923. In doing so, he established the office and role of "the counsel on public relations," a role, he suggested, that should be broadly adopted by companies, governments, and social organizations—and one for which he would be paid handsomely to fill.

His book achieved some early notoriety, and he was invited to counsel Calvin Coolidge on his presidential bid. Specifically, as Bernays related on an entertaining segment of the *David Letterman Show* in 1985, he was asked to find a way to brighten the image of "Cautious Cal." Apparently, shortly before Bernays was brought into the campaign, Alice Roosevelt Longworth—the daughter of Theodore Roosevelt—had popularized the notion that Coolidge was so absent of emotion or humor that he had been "weaned on a pickle" (bottle-fed with vinegar would be more common language, in case any younger readers are finding the concept of weaning on pickles difficult to grasp). The idea that Coolidge had suckled so much pickle juice as an infant that his face was set in a permanent scowl was sticking—to the point that his campaign management felt it could be their undoing.

Bernays was brought in to advise, and he decided the answer was to hold a pancake breakfast on the White House lawn for a host of popular entertainers of the time—singers and dancers, vaudeville performers, and the like. (It's an imaginative idea. Just think of the reaction today if there was a presidential breakfast on the White House lawn that was catered by IHOP and featured Beyoncé, David Blaine, Lin-Manuel Miranda, and the high-kicking Rockettes.) The press, of course, was invited to report on the event, and the *New York Times* headline suggested that "The President Almost Smiled." That glimmer of a smile was enough to shift the polarity of public sentiment. Coolidge went on to win the election.

This brand of headline-grabbing sensationalism became Bernays's stock-in-trade. (And he plied that trade well into his nineties—he was ninety-three years old when he appeared on *Letterman*, and he lived for a decade after that.)

Throughout his career, he engineered several equally successful actions on behalf of politicians and brands. He intercepted the women's liberation movement on behalf of the American Tobacco Company, for example, and encouraged women's rights marchers in New York City to hold up packs of Lucky Strike cigarettes as "torches of freedom" to symbolize their strength, unity, and liberty.

Unfortunately, it may have been this kind of social manipulation that ultimately hindered his acceptance as the father of public relations. (You'd be hard-pressed these days to find a student or practitioner of PR who has read Bernays, for example.) There is something inherently manipulative in his writing and his practices—something of the invisible hand, the social engineer, or the hidden persuader. And that perhaps could come from a view that his sensations were often not connected to a "truth" about the brand or the cause. Lucky Strike cigarettes were not symbols of women's freedom. Coolidge was not a humorous man. But even if Bernays's actions were lacking, his execution and understanding of the role of media generation were not.

And core to that understanding was his recognition of the role of the PR counsel to *make the news*, not just *manage the news*. In his mind, his role was not to write a press release about a new product introduction and pitch the story to his friends and contacts in the media. He wasn't a fixer or an intermediary. His job was to shape (crystallize) the views of the public toward a particular issue. And he would do that by understanding the cultural context surrounding the issue. He would understand the anatomy of the market that was impacted by the issue—what were the subgroups, the micro-communities that had something to gain or lose, and who were the influential voices within those groups. And he would create a talkable moment that would shift perceptions of the group—something that the media would report on, something that people would talk about around the dinner table, which is not so very different from the practices of the commercial, social, and cultural successes that we have reviewed already.

Case in point: in one underreported but pivotal move at the end of 2020, Tesla announced that they had disbanded their corporate communications department. They decided that there was no real benefit to the company in fielding questions from automotive reporters on whether they had fixed the issue with the windscreen glass on the Cybertruck.

And the reality is that they were right. Reporters will write about Tesla because people want to hear about Tesla. They have no choice other than to cover the brand because their readers want to hear about the brand and want to talk about the brand. The truth is that if they don't cover the company, the army of Tesla fans would continue to cover it themselves with their own elaborate systems of information gathering and recreational espionage. And regular readers—or listeners or watchers—of automotive news would simply move to the fan sites and YouTube channels rather than patronizing the traditional purveyors of auto news.

Tesla didn't need to manage the news because they made the news.

Or, as Bernays himself said:

> The Public relations counsel must not only supply news—he must create news. He must lift startling facts from his whole subject and present them as news. He must isolate ideas and develop them into events so that they can be more readily understood and so they can claim attention as news.

Unlike the Ford Motor Company, for example, Tesla doesn't need to send out a press release about its new truck and invite journalists to a booth at the Detroit Auto Show, where they will get a "first look" at the vehicle before regular folk are invited in. That is a process of supplying "news" that the company wants to deliver (whether it is newsworthy or not). Instead, Tesla uses "startling facts" to create news.

Here's a small example of Tesla creating the news. In Super Bowl LV—Chiefs versus Buccaneers—General Motors spent $15 million to buy commercial space that had the potential to reach one hundred million consumers (albeit in a media environment where some of the world's biggest marketers were competing for a share of attention from the same one hundred million consumers with equivalent media budgets).

The day after the Super Bowl, Tesla made a public purchase of bitcoin and announced that it was going to accept the digital currency as payment for its vehicles. Without any supporting marketing spend, they generated five hundred million impressions around the world and solidified their position as the most innovative and inventive automotive manufacturer on the planet.

So, at the same time that Tesla was disbanding its corporate communications department, it continued to demonstrate that it was arguably the most successful corporate communicator in the world.

Although the shuttering of a corporate comms group was, on the surface, a small act (and, in fact, there was very little coverage of it in the marketing or automotive trade press), it was a pivotal moment for the marketing communications industry. It was a signal that the traditional silos and structures that made up the industry no longer worked for them. The corporate communications department wasn't something that they needed to invest in. But, ironically, they had also firmly established that advertising wasn't something they needed to invest in, so PR and earned media were how they were building one of the most powerful and interesting brands in the world. The difference was that they weren't building that brand by relying on a single earned media group within the company; they were building it by recognizing that every action the company made had the potential to earn media.

A shift had happened. And a shift had been recognized. The way brands had been built for the last seventy years of the broadcast era was no longer working for a modern marketer like Tesla. The definition of the marketing services disciplines no longer made structural sense for them. And the muscle memory that corporate marketers the world over were using to support their brands was not a muscle they needed to exercise.

They were marketing in new ways. Building their brand in new ways. And it was working.

Build Your Platform

During those broadcast-era years, the basic job of a marketer or communications professional was to make a connection between their brand and the consumer—a bridge, if you will, between the desires of the company—the brand—and the dreams of the consumer.

The complicating factor here was that all brands had the same basic desire: they wanted an ever-greater share of the category they competed in. And in any category, there were lots of other brands trying to make similar connections, so the category got noisy.

But marketers and their agency partners became adept at finding ways to break through that category clutter. They would analyze the competitive context and determine where they had an edge, a competitive difference, and they would research the beliefs, motivations, and preferences of their customers and potential customers to determine whether that point of differentiation was in some way meaningful to them.

A generation of professionals employed a raft of primary research tools—from focus groups to ethnographic research—to understand how people felt about a brand in relation to its competitors. And brand marketers would fret over the details that would stake a claim to uniqueness within their category: "We've got 10 percent more chocolate." The resulting brand-building activity would frame that uniqueness in a way that was understood to best connect to the consumer's mindset: "Chocolate is an indulgent pleasure." And a "broadcast" campaign would result: "We've got 10 percent more chocolate.... Chocolate is an indulgent pleasure.... A little more to love."

But finding any kind of real competitive difference now is next to impossible. According to an analysis by Joe Mandese, the editor in chief of *MediaPost*, in 1980, there were a mere two hundred national brands in the US. That number had grown to four thousand by 1990. By 2020, there were twelve million national brands in the country.

By any measure, that is hypercompetition, and that degree of competition is only magnified when you consider how quickly product innovation can be copied in any category. So, in the absence of some lock-tight intellectual property—which is hard to find in consumer goods—the search for competitive differentiation is generally a fool's errand.

The context has changed. It's not enough for the brand to concern itself with the noise that's coming from its direct competitors anymore. Often, that's not what's getting in the way of its communication. Instead, the noise that surrounds the brand is the noise of an always-on, often interesting, sometimes overwhelming culture.

We're not competing for share of category anymore. We're competing for share of culture. And to compete successfully, it is essential to understand what makes the brand relevant in the current cultural context.

So, while it's no longer productive to analyze the brand's category to determine where it can best stake a claim, it is becoming important for the brand to analyze its cultural context to find a place where it can play.

Understanding the cultural relevance of a brand is becoming central to generating conversation that aligns with the brand's truth. There are a million different cultural conversations going on at any given time—some important on a macro, geopolitical level and others quite trivial by comparison. But understanding which of them the brand can authentically lean into can make the difference between success and failure.

Nike's support for Colin Kaepernick in the midst of the BLM movement was a prime example of authentically connecting to a cultural conversation. Nike's ethos of the athlete above all else made it natural that they would continue to support Kaepernick as the NFL turned its back on him. And the cultural position they took, that you should "stand for something even if it costs you everything," perfectly aligned the values and stance of the player with the Nike brand.

Contrast that, however, with the Pepsi advertisement featuring Kendall Jenner resolving the tension surrounding a BLM protest by handing a police officer a can of Pepsi—an entirely tone-deaf example of misunderstanding the cultural context and shoehorning a brand into a conversation it didn't belong in.

Importantly for planning, the cultural platform isn't something that is fixed and permanent like the brand's truth—it is something that should be fluid, changing to move with the currents of the cultural conversation and not getting bogged down in a conversation that has already moved on.

Tactically speaking, a good rule of thumb would be to reassess the cultural platform every quarter to determine whether it still holds, whether it has moved on, or whether there is an adjacent conversation that offers more potential for the brand to drive conversation.

And in articulating the cultural platform, it's useful to think about another shift from the broadcast-era positioning statement.

Traditional brand positioning statements tend to be written as statements of uniqueness or superiority. Declarations, if you like. And when the requirement was to broadcast a point of brand differentiation, that was fine.

But the requirement of brand communication in the Attention Economy is to drive conversation, participation, and engagement. To that end, the cultural platform should be written as an invitation rather than a declaration.

For illustration, think about the famous tagline for British Airways: "The world's favorite airline." As a controlled message in paid media, it was excellent—a defining, long-running statement of uniqueness and superiority. But it won't start a conversation (beyond perhaps asking the question, "Is it?").

Compare that with a culturally relevant invitation from REI to "opt outside" on Black Friday—to forgo the checkout lines and do with REI gear what you're meant to do with REI gear: explore nature. It naturally elicits conversation on several levels, from the media shock and awe that a retailer would shut its doors on the biggest shopping day of the year to the thumbs-up, stick-it-to-the-man support from fans of the brand.

The cultural platform is a piece of language that can anchor all the activities that surround a cultural conversation the brand is engaging in. The goal is for it to be memorable, to align with the brand's truth, and to provide an invitation to participate. Which is simple to say and one of the most difficult jobs to do in the world of creative communications. The elegant simplicity of a phrase like "opt outside" or "let's motor" is the gold, frankincense, and myrrh of creative communications. It is the "K-Line" that connects all the brand's activities together over a certain period.

Again, unlike the brand's truth, the brand's cultural platform doesn't need to be consistent. It does need to consistently reflect the brand's truth, but the platform itself can change over time. In fact, it almost certainly should change over time to avoid becoming stale and uninteresting.

If the truth of the brand is made up of some unchanging combination of its philosophy and its personality, then the talkability of the brand is driven by its platform. The cultural tension it is trying to resolve. The cultural conversation that it can authentically participate in and contribute to.

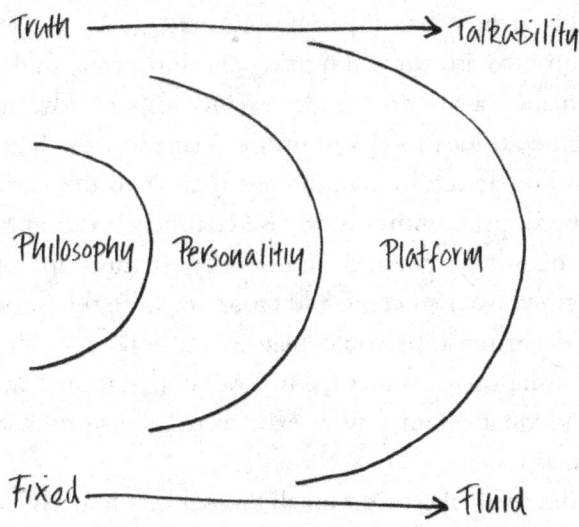

On one level, it relies on nothing more sophisticated than great strategic and creative talent to achieve. However, one surefire way of generating a platform that has the potential for creative publicity is to put creative people in the same room with publicists while the work is being created.

For the sake of absolute clarity here, creatives are the copywriters and art directors who make up the words-and-pictures partnership of creative teams, and publicists are the traditional, social, and influencer media teams that sit within earned media agencies.

Paradoxically, it's not common for those groups to mingle. Often, in agency settings, there is a baton-pass moment between the creative teams and the channel teams, with the latter having had little voice in the development of the work they are being asked to publicize. But when the teams work together, the whole is invariably greater than the sum of its parts.

A good media team will quickly and intuitively understand how "mediable" a story or an idea is, and, importantly, they can help reframe an idea to give it greater earned-media legs. They will assess how much human interest there is in the story; how many subgroups, communities, and channels it can appeal to; whether there is potential for a celebrity partnership; whether influencer involvement could add more weight to the story; what role brand partnerships could play in the rollout of the campaign; whether there is potential to cover both national and local media; and what opportunities exist to tell the story in emerging channels.

And they will take a view on all those things fast! The result is that the speed of development is accelerated, and the larger team doesn't get bogged down in developing an idea that is fundamentally flawed in its ability to generate coverage and engagement.

Be Everywhere, All the Time

Once a cultural platform is established, the next task is to bring it to life in the world—to give it energy and create conversation and engagement around it.

Energy is an often-overlooked principle in marketing. In the broadcast era, it wasn't required. For the sake of simplicity, an advertising agency would often develop a campaign of three TV commercials that would run for an entire year before they were deemed to have worn out and the planning process would begin again. It was almost the opposite of energetic. Visible, yes. But energetic, no.

Interestingly, though, two advertising agencies, Y&R and DDB, fielded parallel studies that yielded a common finding on the importance of brand energy.

One from Y&R was called the Brand Asset Valuator (it's still going and still relevant today, although the agency name Y&R has been lost to history). The other from DDB was called the Brand Capital study. Importantly, although they were conducted by different people employing different theories and methodologies, both had a finding in common: a brand's "energy" was a significant contributor to a brand's health.

The Y&R study stated that brand energy is a leading predictor of usage and preference and that it added an incremental 64 percent to brand value than did sales growth alone. The DDB study showed that (like Ehrenberg's Dirichlet model) the number of people who loved a brand grew in exponential proportion to the number of people who liked a brand. (The more people like you, the more they will love you.) And it found that the dimension that was most predictive of brand love was brand growth, defined as a combination of energy and dynamism (rather than physical sales growth).

Energy is a powerful force—both in the physical and the marketing worlds. And yet, the broadcast-era marketer can often either fail to acknowledge that or actively work against it.

An old story in the annals of advertising history had it that Rosser Reeves, who was the co-founder and eventual chairman of an agency called Ted Bates, was entertaining a client aboard his yacht, when the client turned to Reeves and challenged: "You have seventy-six people working on my account, and yet we have run the same commercial for five years. What are they all doing?" (I have an inexplicable urge to write the words "Damn you, man" at the end of that quote and read it in the voice of Anthony Hopkins…) Reeves's reply was succinct. He simply said, "They are working flat out to stop your people changing it."

Perhaps that strategy was sensible in the 1950s. It was certainly shown to work at the time, when single commercials written by Reeves could generate vast amounts of revenue for his clients—even though they were considered grating and annoying by regular folk.

But in those days, there was no off switch for annoying commercials. You couldn't really even change the channel because there weren't many, so you'd likely put up with a moment's annoyance for the benefit of the wholesome and free entertainment that followed it.

But that strategy would clearly not work now.

In any digital media, the advertisement would likely be skipped, and if for some reason it wasn't, the relentless repetition of a single commercial would create the impression of a brand in decline.

In the Attention Economy, brands need to demonstrate their energy by being engaged, connected to culture, and visible in multiple mediums simultaneously. In the Attention Economy, everything is media. We don't make media choices anymore. We choose everything. We consume more media than ever before, but we rarely concentrate our attention on any one thing at one time. So, to achieve any degree of success, brands must think holistically about the effect all their communication has on their potential new customers.

Price is a medium, and the price a brand charges sends a message. The blankets may be the most important medium Virgin Atlantic employs, and the materials they choose for their blankets may be the most important message they can send. The way a service representative answers the phone, the way the brand responds to a comment in its Instagram feed, the way a salesperson approaches a retailer, the way the delivery driver drives, the signage on the side of the truck, whether the truck is clean or not—every single thing, from the smallest to the largest, says something about the brand. And the brand needs to have the energy to stay proactively, creatively, and consistently engaged across all those mediums and all those opportunities to connect with new potential customers.

All the examples we looked at earlier do that. Whether BTS or Trump, they appear ubiquitous, relentless, unsleeping, untiring. But that is what is required of a successful brand in the Attention Economy.

Importantly, this reinforces the need for brands to be consistent in every aspect of their presence and their presentation. It's simply not enough for brands to run the same television commercial repeatedly in the name of consistency. (That will likely achieve a different result.) Instead, they need a sense of self that is clear enough for multiple people in multiple departments and multiple external agencies to create ceaseless energy in their marketing that all feels like it's coming from the same place.

Develop an Editorial Calendar

The content or editorial calendar is the backbone of earned-media storytelling and is how the brand can ensure a base level of coverage and conversational energy. It also provides a degree of structure that is essential when a brand is operating with ubiquitous energy.

The calendar relies on a structured plan of activity with peaks of excitement throughout the year, combined with a steady drumbeat of "interesting" in support.

The excitement comes from macro brand activities—meaningful product launches, brand experiences, content series, or new partnerships, for example. Ideally, they would be spaced with a manageable cadence throughout the year—one every two or three months, for example. The reason for that spacing is that the activity shouldn't be viewed as a single, point-in-time event, but rather the pinnacle moment in a coordinated sequence of activity. Think of it as an on-ramp to the activity, followed by a long tail.

Movie launches offer a good example of this type of planning. Many months before the actual "event," news will start to be distributed. The stars will be announced, trailers released, theme songs teased, glimpses of behind-the-scenes action shared (some of them tailored for specific outlets). Stories about budget overruns will be leaked, budding relationships between the stars rumored, and on-set injuries reported.

The launch of the movie itself will be anchored by a red-carpet premiere with all the stars in attendance. A media roadshow will follow, with the stars and possibly the director on tour to talk to various media outlets about the film. Then, a long tail of post-launch activity will be encouraged. A limited theatrical release will turn into a national release, which will be followed by an eagerly awaited streaming date. Those budding romances will start to flower—or wilt. The backstories of the production will be told in interviews. Merchandise will drop—franchised toys, posters, apparel. And after a while, the conversation will move on to something new.

Movies offer an obvious example of the on-ramp and the long tail. Consumer technology brands are equally good at employing the approach—think about the launch of a new iPhone, for example. But any brand activity that is intrinsically interesting can apply the same planning construct.

Plan and Pivot

If big brand excitement is driven by macro moments, the steady drumbeat comes from the micro. There was a time when brands developing a social media strategy thought about an "always-on" approach to their communications. But in real terms, there is a danger that an "always-on" mentality can lead to activity for the sake of activity. A better mindset is to shift from "always on" to "always interesting." And the best way to achieve that is to actively seek out moments of cultural opportunity.

Every day, opportunities will arise to insert the brand into the cultural conversation, to recognize and amplify cultural energy when it naturally appears. Skilled listening to social and traditional media channels will surface those opportunities. The key to taking advantage of them, though, is to have the mindset and infrastructure in place to act quickly.

Often, the move from conversation to participation will happen on the same day. Sometimes that participation will be as simple as a tweet or a comment on Reddit. Sometimes it will require actual production. The determination on whether there is time to wait for something to be produced will often come down to a judgment on how long the conversation will continue.

Jumping quickly into a social conversation can yield significant results for a brand. A recent, lovable example came from McDonald's, which celebrated the birthday of its furry, purple mascot, Grimace, by having him throw the first pitch in the baseball game between the New York Mets and the Miami Marlins.

It was June 12, and at that point in the season, the Mets were struggling with a 29-37 win/loss record and had only managed eight wins in their previous twenty games. But when they broke their losing streak that day, something magical started to happen.

Social listening picked up early signs of an emerging narrative as fans began crediting Grimace with the victory. Early posts came from influential voices in the baseball community.

> I'm telling you right now Mets are gonna go on a run. Grimace is a major good luck charm. Bet Mets tonight big, thank me later.

> Mets are now 5-0 since Grimace threw out the first pitch.

> The grimace effect is REAL #LGM

> Grimace has changed the course of Mets history forever.

By June 17, the "effect" was cementing itself in popular culture, and mainstream media began to take notice. *GQ* asked, "Can Grimace Save the Mets' Season?" ESPN and *Forbes* quickly followed suit, and the cultural echo chamber began manufacturing memes.

McDonald's understood that they didn't need to create the story—fans were already doing that. They simply needed to fuel it. Rather than trying to control the narrative through traditional paid media, they set out to amplify the wave of fan-driven conversation in ways that felt authentic to both brands.

Within days, they had collaborated with the Mets to have Grimace take over McDonald's social media, they converted their profile pictures to show Grimace in a Mets cap, they shifted their entire social tone to match Grimace's voice, they placed Grimace billboards at the Mets' ballpark, and importantly, they started responding to fans directly to fuel the conversation.

When fans began showing up to games in bootleg Grimace costumes, the team didn't try to police it—they celebrated it. When one fan in a Grimace costume was caught on camera chugging a beer during a rain delay, the moment went viral. The McDonald's team amplified it rather than worrying about brand safety. They understood that in the Attention Economy, authenticity trumps control.

The campaign demonstrated how organic cultural moments can snowball when brands fuel them properly. When the Empire State Building's social team slid into McDonald's DMs, the team seized the opportunity. Within days, they had flown Grimace to NYC for a party at the top of the Empire State Building, gathered key city influencers and superfans for the event, and coordinated to light the building's spire in Grimace purple.

Each activation built on the one before it, creating a virtuous cycle of earned media and fan engagement. The team kept the momentum going by continually finding new ways to celebrate the fandom, including installing a permanent purple "Grimace seat" at Citi Field—the first-ever permanent brand fixture in the stadium.

The results demonstrated the power of moving at the speed of culture. McDonald's became the most talked-about brand in NYC throughout the summer. They gained more than three times the share of cultural conversation versus competitors. The story generated over 3,500 earned media placements across major outlets. They earned thirty-seven thousand social mentions without spending on paid media. And the campaign fueled significant sales growth in NYC and beyond.

But perhaps most tellingly, the campaign's impact extended far beyond the initial activation. Grimace's status as the Mets' unofficial mascot became permanently embedded in the cultural fabric of the team. The purple seat at Citi Field stands as a permanent reminder of a moment when a brand recognized and amplified authentic cultural energy.

This wasn't a campaign that could have been planned. It required an organization that was designed to spot organic cultural energy when it emerged, with an active social listening infrastructure in place, empowered teams who could flag potential opportunities quickly, and a native understanding of the cultural context that could recognize significant trends fast. They also had to be agile enough to act on those trends quickly, with decision-making processes that could move at the speed of culture and creative and production capabilities tuned for fast action. They had to be patient enough to let fans help shape the narrative, willing to take calculated risks, and patient enough to let the story unfold at its own pace—amplifying where appropriate but not trying to force the cadence.

The success of the Grimace Effect demonstrates that in the Attention Economy, the ability to plan and pivot—to recognize and amplify authentic cultural moments—can be more powerful than even the most carefully orchestrated traditional campaign. The key is building an organization that's ready to move at the speed of culture when those moments arise.

This represents a fundamental shift from broadcast-era marketing, where campaigns were meticulously planned and messages carefully controlled. In the Attention Economy, while planning remains important, it's equally crucial to develop the capability to recognize and amplify organic cultural energy when it emerges.

The brands that win are the ones that can balance both—maintaining clear brand purpose and guidelines while being nimble enough to join cultural conversations in authentic ways. They understand that some of their most powerful moments may come not from their own careful plans, but from their ability to recognize and amplify the natural cultural energy that emerges around their brand.

The Grimace Effect joins a host of successful plan-and-pivot moments that have defined Attention-Economy marketing. One early and famous example came during Super Bowl XLVII in 2013, when the Mercedes-Benz Superdome experienced a thirty-four-minute power outage. Oreo's social media team capitalized on the moment with a simple tweet showing an Oreo cookie against a dark background with the caption, "Power out? No problem. You can still dunk in the dark." The tweet garnered over fifteen thousand retweets and six thousand favorites within hours.

But what's often overlooked about the Oreo moment is the infrastructure that enabled it. The brand had assembled a fifteen-person "command center" of creative and social media professionals ready to respond to Super Bowl moments in real time. They had clear approval processes in place that allowed them to move from idea to execution in minutes. The tweet wasn't just lucky—it was the result of deliberate organizational preparation to capitalize on cultural moments.

A more sustained example came from Aviation Gin in 2019, when they responded to a Peloton ad that sparked widespread controversy. On the surface, it was a simple holiday commercial showing a husband gifting his wife one of their bikes, but the subtext was troubling, with clear sexist and misogynistic undertones that viewers reacted to loudly. Within seventy-two hours, Aviation Gin had created and released a response ad featuring the same actress, now drinking gin with friends who tell her she's "safe here." The ad garnered over ten million views on Twitter alone.

What made the Aviation Gin response particularly effective was that it didn't just piggyback on a trending topic—it advanced the cultural conversation. Just as McDonald's didn't try to control the Grimace narrative but instead amplified existing fan energy, Aviation Gin tapped into authentic cultural sentiment rather than trying to manufacture it.

More recent examples show how this rapid-response capability has evolved. When OpenAI CEO Sam Altman was suddenly fired and then rehired in November 2023, Duolingo's social media team captured attention with a series of perfectly timed posts. As the drama unfolded, they posted "duo has not been fired," followed by "duo has not been rehired," and finally, "duo is staying besties." The posts garnered hundreds of thousands of likes and significant media coverage, not because they were particularly clever but because they demonstrated cultural fluency—understanding both the moment and how their audience was processing it.

The M&M's brand demonstrated similar instincts during the 2024 Super Bowl. After a year of manufactured controversy around their spokes-candies, including a publicity stunt where they were "indefinitely paused" in favor of Maya Rudolph, they used the big game to announce a fake campaign for "candy-coated clam bites." The intentionally absurd activation generated significant earned media, but more importantly, it showed how brands can turn cultural criticism into cultural capital when they understand the conversation.

Even traditionally conservative brands have learned to move at the speed of culture. When Taylor Swift began attending Kansas City Chiefs games to support Travis Kelce in 2023, United Airlines quickly added flight numbers 1989 (referencing Swift's album) and 87 (Kelce's number) to their routes between New York and Kansas City. They followed this by adding "Taylor's Version" to their onboard safety speech and renaming menu items with Swift song titles. These weren't expensive activations, but they demonstrated real cultural fluency and earned significant media attention.

What makes these recent examples particularly noteworthy is how they balance speed with strategy. Rather than simply jumping on trending topics, they found authentic ways to participate in cultural conversations that aligned with their brand truth. United's activations worked because they enhanced the customer experience while joining a cultural conversation. M&M's clam campaign worked because it showed self-awareness while staying true to the brand's playful personality.

But what the Grimace example demonstrates best is that although these opportunities are sparked in the moment, with the right fuel—in the form of well-designed communications infrastructure, cultural intuition, and a clear understanding of the brand's truth—they can continue to burn.

By repeatedly finding new ways to fuel the conversation—from social engagement to physical activations to permanent installations—they extended what could have been a brief viral moment into lasting cultural impact.

Integrate Your Earned Media

The traditional practice of generating media coverage is indelibly connected to the PR industry (all the way back to Edward Bernays). And the practice of earning media has long been associated with the practices of the PR professional: the press release, the media tour, the "smile and dial" pitching of stories to beat reporters. (Indeed, for PR professionals, the words "earned media" still relate directly to coverage generated in traditional media outlets.)

However, while the "walled garden of journalistic influence" that defined and demanded those traditional PR skills has wilted, new outlets for earned media and earned-media practices have bloomed.

The twenty-four-hour news cycle has created an insatiable demand for content, stories, and news from traditional media owners. The rise of the social-media influencer, with their Instagram followings and Twitch channels, has created an avalanche of new micro-media owners, all eager for something new to talk about and all feeding off one another in an echo chamber of content and conversation.

As we have seen, many modern businesses realized they could build a brand themselves in this new media environment without relying on traditional advertising or paid media execution. Some of those brands were the digitally native, vertically integrated unicorns created by the technology infrastructure of the mobile web—Airbnb, Uber, and Warby Parker. But others in more traditional categories did the same. Neither Zara, Trader Joe's, nor

Krispy Kreme, for example, built its brand through traditional advertising, and yet all of them have built objectively powerful brands—Zara ranked at number forty-five on Interbrand's list of most powerful global brands, ahead of Dior and Burberry.

What this non-traditional brand building required, though, was a new model of earned media execution: an integrated, brand-led approach to earned media that connects all the earned disciplines and channels together. One that applies the same skills and principles of generating talkability to traditional PR outlets as well as to influencer marketing, organic social media, community management, content marketing, experiential marketing, and so on. And one that does it all through the lens of the brand's truth.

Interestingly, there are still many traditional marketing and communications organizations that don't integrate their earned media disciplines. (Even at the most fundamental level, many brands still separate the responsibility for PR from organic social media and influencer marketing into different departments with different budgets.) But more progressive brands and agencies are recognizing this disconnect and have structured themselves to operate more holistically.

The interplay between traditional and social media channels is fluid and constant. Sixteen percent of traditional media journalists get their news from X/Twitter, and 58 percent check brand social channels when reporting. In the last two years alone, traffic to news-media websites from social channels has increased by 31 percent. And a full 53 percent of us now get our news from social media.

It's clear that the days when traditional, digital, social, and influencer media teams can sit in silos are behind us. To effectively coordinate a brand's earned media activity, an omni-channel planning approach needs to be in place.

There are two principles that can guide the successful development of an integrated earned media plan:

1. Start with the consumer, not the media.
2. Structure the phasing of your media campaign.

In many ways, this should seem self-evident, particularly to marketers who are used to working in a paid-media environment, where there have long been media-optimization models with consumer data at their core. But in the earned-media world, it has been difficult to apply the same level of data-based rigor to media selection, and often, the media outlet is considered a "proxy" for the consumer. Therefore, it will be assumed that home chefs will watch Bobby Flay on HGTV, for example. And while they may, that may not be the best way to engage with them.

Increasingly, however, earned-media teams have access to the kind of first-party data that their paid-media counterparts have long been used to. And the analysis of that data is leading them to reconsider how to most efficiently engage with various consumer groups.

A simple way to prioritize channels is to consider the role the channel plays in relation to the objectives of a campaign. Does it offer depth of engagement, or does it offer breadth of reach? There are few outlets that do both, and understanding the distinction between them—and why you might use one rather than the other—becomes important.

Different channels will play different roles in a campaign lifecycle, and understanding those roles will help effectively integrate an omnichannel earned-media campaign. Consider the following campaign cadence, for example:

Eight weeks out from launch, the full media team would be briefed at the same time as the creative team, who would be tasked with developing supporting content alongside any influencer partnerships that were under consideration. An integrated channel plan would be created, and the primary media and channel partners would be contacted to be given the inside track on the story.

Six weeks out, the on-ramp seeding of the story would begin across traditional and social channels, with exclusive content being offered to core media partners. Influencer partnerships would be contracted, and any content requirements from those partnerships would begin to be co-created.

Four weeks out, target media channels would be input into the brand's social/cultural listening system, and the conversation would be actively monitored on a daily basis for opportunities to insert the brand into the cultural conversation of the time.

Two weeks out, work would accelerate with primary channel partners to develop their embargoed launch-day story.

On launch day, all created content would go live on brand social channels at the same time as the embargoed stories go live across primary media targets. Influencers would go live with co-created content. Links would be shared to media partners and influencer posts to encourage cross-channel engagement, and the brand's community management team would begin to actively engage with conversations on brand and partner channels.

Three days post-launch, the best-performing content from the launch (including coverage from top-tier media partners) would be assessed for boosting through paid-media amplification. Social listening would continue for the potential for opportunistic engagement, and a second round of co-created influencer content would go live.

And after seven days, the best-performing content from the brand, influencers, and top-tier media would again be considered for potential paid amplification. All the while, social listening and cultural opportunism would continue.

Dance Like No One's Watching

The most fundamental shift in mindset required to generate creative publicity for a brand is to stop intruding on the entertainment and become the entertainment. And while being the entertainment in this new media environment requires something of an attitude shift, it also requires a healthy disrespect for convention and a willingness to flaunt the rules.

To become the entertainment rather than intrude on it means that companies must let their guard down. They need to seed ideas and see which flourish. They must embrace the thought that people may like their idea so much that they will want to create their own version of it. Ultimately, they've got to be comfortable enough with their own brand to have fun with it. And when they are, they will see that we all embrace anyone who can make us smile when we wouldn't otherwise.

Peter Sagan did that effortlessly.

Sagan was a professional cyclist (arguably the world's most exciting cyclist at the time) who announced his retirement from road racing at the end of the 2023 season. Until recently, he had more followers than the Tour de France—the most-watched sporting event of any kind anywhere. A 2024 profile in *Bicycling* magazine described him in ways not ordinarily associated with cyclists: "He was luminous. He was brash, exciting, and electrifying."

He seemed capable of anything: he could climb, he could sprint, he could perform in time trials, and he was a terrifyingly good descender. But his popularity didn't rest solely on an objective view of his cycling prowess. One of his longtime friends described him this way: "Also, there's the way he likes to ride with his heart. Sometimes, that goes against achieving your goal. But I think that's also why people love him so much."

Sagan rode with flair. Cycling was a performance for him. He regularly pulled wheelies in races—happily riding uphill on one wheel. (He once signed a copy of his autobiography while climbing a mountain stage of a Grand Tour.) And he spoke his mind. He knew who he was and what he stood for, and he was clear about it. Often provocative, always entertaining. Peter Sagan was, and is, an important brand in cycling. In that, he exemplifies the marketing mindset that creates success in the Attention Economy. And it is not salesmanship. Instead, it is closer to the words that best describe Sagan: "luminous, brash, exciting, and electrifying."

What Sagan did so artfully and successfully was direct a disproportionate amount of the cultural conversation around cycling and road racing toward himself. And he did it by employing two principles that should guide the activities of any Attention-Economy marketer:

1. He was provocative.
2. He was an engaging guest.

Provocation is the lifeblood of the Attention Economy. We read it, we react to it, we encourage it—whether we want to or not.

Provocation adds volume to your voice, and in the Attention Economy, "the loudest voices are the ones with the most power."

But when we think about provocative actions, particularly in this cultural moment, we are likely to view them in a negative light. Indeed, some dictionaries are entirely one-sided in their use of the word. Macmillan, for example, defines *provocative* as, "intended to start arguments between people or to make people angry or upset."

And provocation has undoubtedly become a political tool that has been wielded to great effect to make people angry and upset, often by sowing division and spreading disinformation. But provocation needn't be thought about in those terms. "A thoughtful and provocative book" is not one that seeks to titillate, divide, or make people angry. "A provocative idea" in an academic setting is one that sparks new thought, not one that seeks to spark division. Webster defines *provocative* as, "serving or tending to provoke, excite, or stimulate." A scattering of synonyms for the word includes "edgy," "exciting," and "stimulating." And for brands seeking to appeal to a broad universe of buyers, it is important that they are edgy, exciting, and stimulating—or like Peter Sagan, "brash, exciting, and electrifying."

For Attention-Economy marketers, the key to the appropriate use of provocation is to study the cultural currents that flow around your brand and to find ways to create edgy, exciting, or stimulating connections to them—but importantly, to do so in a way that feels true to your brand.

We touched on a good example of this from Nike. One of their most effective marketing actions of the last few years was also—unsurprisingly—their most provocative: the endorsement of NFL quarterback Colin Kaepernick.

Kaepernick played six seasons for the San Francisco 49ers before being famously sidelined for taking a knee to protest police brutality and racial inequality while the national anthem was being played. His actions provoked significant debate among players, politicians, and the league, and he maintained that he was being blackballed as a result.

Kaepernick had been a Nike-sponsored athlete since 2011, and during the controversy, there was a serious discussion within the company to end the deal. But their global head of communications fought to keep the contract alive, and at the urging of their advertising agency, they stood behind Kaepernick.

Their stance felt in every way true to the Nike brand ethos. Kaepernick's belief in his cause mirrored Phil Knight's devotion to his company: *Seek a calling. Even if you don't know what that means, seek it. If you're following your calling, the fatigue will be easier to bear, the disappointments will be fuel, the highs will be like nothing you've ever felt.* Since their earliest days and their relationship with the mercurial track star Steve Prefontaine, Nike had always been comfortable standing with the maverick. And so, while its brand action was clearly provocative, it wasn't provocation in the service of division or negativity. It didn't feel opportunistic. And it worked.

The campaign launched on Labor Day with a post on Kaepernick's Twitter account with the hashtag #JustDoIt. Beautiful and provocative advertising ran with the line, "Believe in something. Even if it means sacrificing everything." Other prominent Nike athletes—in particular, Serena Williams and LeBron James—quickly voiced their support on social media, and the conversation exploded.

According to social media tracking firm Talkwalker, social mentions of the brand jumped 1,400 percent in a day. Within three days, the Apex Marketing Group had valued the earned media exposure of the campaign at $163 million. The brand also attracted 170,000 new followers on Instagram. Online sales for the month increased by 31 percent.

But the gamble had been real. The day after the campaign broke, Nike's stock declined by 3.2 percent—a drop of hundreds of millions of dollars in market capitalization. And yet, within two weeks, their share price had rebounded to an all-time high. According to the *New York Times*, "The campaign had yielded 'record engagement with the brand.'…quickly becoming among the most talked-about and successful campaigns in recent years."[42]

So, provocation can clearly work to get noticed in the Attention Economy. But importantly, the provocation must be true to your brand, and it must be something that your customers and potential customers get value from.

> If you're going to invite yourself into someone's home, you have a duty not to bore them or insult them by shouting at them. On the other hand, if you can make them smile or show them something interesting or enjoyable—if you're a charming guest—then they may like you a bit better, and then they may be more likely to buy your product. (Martin Boase)

Martin Boase was one of the founders of the fabled British advertising agency BMP. He had a notable focus on "profits after performance" in business, and that instinct helped create an agency that developed some of the best-loved advertising campaigns in the UK (a poll in 2000 found that of the top one hundred campaigns in Britain, sixteen had been produced by BMP). BMP was a product of what was being called the creative revolution in the US, and a fair summary of the approach that advertising school took to their craft was to be viewed as a "charming guest" in the homes of the people their work entered. And that principle holds true today.

If we want to be included in a conversation, we need to be provocative. We need to be edgy, exciting, and stimulating. But if we want to be invited to the party, we need to be good guests. This is where the art of marketing and communications comes into play.

The creative revolution in American advertising was sparked by an agency called Doyle Dane Bernbach, which was founded in 1949 by Bill Bernbach. The agency had artistry at its core, and its operating premise stood in stark contrast to the other advertising giants of the time, who backed the science of marketing and reinforced the importance of research and measurability. Bernbach, on the other hand, believed that the only thing of real value in advertising was artistry. *Is creativity some obscure, esoteric art form? Not on your life. It's the most practical thing a business[man] can employ.*

Although standing against the view that creativity was obscure or esoteric, Bernbach did recognize its intangibility. Returning to the distinction between feeling and thinking, he wrote:

> You can turn a page and, before you really comprehend it, there's a feeling. There's a vibration. If it's the wrong vibration for what you want to convey, what follows is going to fight it—an uphill battle against the original impression you made.

(I'm not sure whether this is true, but one of my favorite stories from the history of DDB is that one of their famous art directors—a man by the name of Helmut Krone—reportedly told one of his copywriters, "I can sell more with pink than you can with all of your words.") Strangely, the importance of creativity remains in debate today, seventy years after Bernbach opened shop. However, you won't be surprised by now to hear that Binet and Field have weighed in on the topic, pointing out that creatively awarded campaigns are more effective in driving market share than campaigns that did not win awards.

Creativity is unquestionably a powerful force in marketing, and even if we think about our own lives and the way we connect with ideas, images, or content, the joyful surprise of a creative act is what makes a brand or a person an engaging guest. It's what gets you invited to the party.

That becomes more important as more and more of our marketing and communications effort is being directed online—simply because, as that happens, our communications are being consumed in an interactive medium. Yes, interactive. (Some of you may remember that the internet was called an interactive medium when marketers first began exploring its potential.)

When we're in an interactive space, we don't want to be confronted with linear, persuasive, controlled messages. They feel out of place, out of context. When we see something, we want to comment on it, we want to share it, we want to make a meme out of it, we want to retweet it.

We don't want to just view it (like on TV); we want to be part of it. We don't want controlled communication from brands. We want to control the communication from brands.

Broadcast-era creative content tends to follow a narrative arc. The narrative arc is a storytelling device that forms the basis of nearly all TV shows, movies, novels, comic books, and so on. The arc follows a simple pattern that leads the audience through a story in a digestible and familiar way. It is often structured into three acts: beginning, middle, and end. The beginning features an inciting incident, something that sparks the events that follow. Those events then build to a central tension, often leading to a climax in the drama. And finally, the tension is resolved. Boy meets girl. Boy loses girl. Boy gets girl back again.

From long-copy print ads to thirty-second TV commercials, stories have followed this form. Incidents were incited, and tensions were resolved. Neat little stories wrapped in tidy bows. After all, "the best part of waking up is Folgers in your cup."

But the big diversion from the broadcast era is the simple recognition that people want to interact with the media they consume. They want to participate. And, therefore, long-term brand-building activities need to allow for—and encourage—that participation from consumers. We want to resolve the tension ourselves. (Or maybe we just want to let the tension build.) We're not looking for all the acts to be laid out neatly for us. Instead, we become engaged by the inciting incident. And we take it from there.

Think about Doggface again. Riding his longboard, sipping Ocean Spray, and listening to Fleetwood Mac. There is no tension in that first video. There certainly is no resolution. But there is a brilliantly incongruous, illogical, charming inciting incident. Something we've never seen before. Lots of things we are familiar with, but all of them in unfamiliar contexts. All of them mushed together to form a beautifully illogical whole. Longboards and Ocean Spray. Head tattoos and Fleetwood Mac. None of it made sense. But it earned our attention, and we all began to participate in, and ultimately complete, the story.

The music video is a prime example of the shift from a broadcast to an Attention-Economy mindset. With the rise of MTV, the music video quickly morphed from simple performances of songs to complex and expensively produced mini-movies—stories with clear narrative arcs and established acts. But increasingly, music videos have become opportunities to incite participation rather than tell a complete story.

The master of the form may be Drake. He is the most-streamed artist in the world and may also hold the title of being the most-memed artist in the world—and it's something he actively encourages. In an interview with Instagram, he told them:

> I love that I'm the guy that doesn't take himself too seriously. I like laughing even if it's at my expense. It doesn't feel like it's necessarily malicious or hurtful stuff. I'm conscious of it.
>
> I really enjoy it more than watching television. It brings joy to my life. I hope it brings joy to other people's lives too.

One example of his art is the "Hotline Bling" video—notable for its sparse and colorfully graphic set design, but more importantly for the incongruously "grandpa" dance moves. The video was tweeted about over 1.4 million times in its first four weeks, peaking with 350,000 or so tweets per day. Many of the tweets referenced the avalanche of memes and parodies created within the first twenty-four hours of the video's release.

Drake's mastery of earning the public's attention hasn't been for naught. Aside from being a quadruple-platinum recording artist, he's a major global brand with interests in alcoholic beverages, apparel collaborations, and sports team ownership. And as of 2025, he had an estimated net worth of $250 million.

Beyond the music video, music itself has changed. The nature of songwriting has changed. We used to be happy to be led gently into the story of a song. We would be happy to wait for the tension, and we would expect a resolution of that tension. But now we want the tension right away. Songwriters today know they must start the song with "the hook." They can't wait to introduce it; they have to lead with it.

We look for the inciting incident. Then we'll resolve it ourselves. We just want the hook. That's what makes us engaging guests in a modern media context. Don't close the loop; just give me the hook.

Make Advertising Earned First

Consistent with the principles of marketing evolution, it's important to recognize that there are, of course, times when brands have to, want to, or should pay other media owners for their audiences. So, it's important to be clear here that this book (and the concepts of Attention-Economy marketing) is not a repudiation of advertising or of paid media. Paid media advertising that focuses on brand building (rather than simple performance) isn't going away—nor should it, for companies with marketing budgets large enough to afford it.

But equally important is the need to maximize the effect of that paid media by ensuring that it will generate earned media too.

When a brand reaches a scale of distribution that extends beyond the reach of groups of like-minded people, it will inevitably use paid media outlets to energize the brand. Jeff Bezos, who

once stated that "advertising is a tax you pay for a lack of innovation," is now one of the world's largest advertisers. Amazon
is simply too big not to advertise. At some point, some brands
will become big enough that they cannot rely solely on earned,
shared, and owned media to grow their market share. At that
point, they will need to pay for audiences to supplement the
audience they can earn. (That point will come earlier for brands
that are poor at earning the attention of their audience and later
for brands that are good at it.)

We can derive a simple measure of that inflection point
from the broadcast-era toolkit of the Ehrenberg-Bass Institute.
In their research, they determined that when a brand's share of
voice (its relative share of advertising expenditure compared to
its direct competitors) was greater than its share of market, the
brand would grow.

It's a blunt tool, but one that has been made extensive use of
by the paid-media disciplines for many years. Clearly, though,
it has very little relevance for an Attention-Economy marketer.
However, if you substitute the idea of share of voice with that of
share of conversation (the combined effect of both the brand's
paid impressions and its earned impressions across all media),
then the calculation has more relevance.

If, for example, a politician has a materially greater share of
conversation than share of vote (like Donald Trump in the 2016
race for the presidential nomination), there is little need for them
to rely heavily on paid media. On the other hand, a politician in
the same race with a materially lower share of conversation (take
Jeb Bush, for example) would need to rely heavily on paid media
to make up the deficit. In that instance, as we saw, the delta in
share of conversation was just too great to be bridged with Jeb's

paid media budgets—even when those paid media budgets were significantly larger than Trump's.

So, once again, this isn't a repudiation of advertising or paid media; rather, it is an exhortation to think about the fundamental role that advertising plays—which (as Andrew Ehrenberg and Paul Feldwick have taught us) is to generate creative publicity that will result in fame and popularity for a brand. And, therefore, it is an exhortation to concern ourselves with the central question, "Will this advertising get talked about?" before it is approved or produced.

The reality is that very little advertising gets talked about anymore. The days of celebrating ads like the Cadbury Gorilla drumming to a Phil Collins tune feel a long way behind us. There are exceptions, of course. In the US, Super Bowl advertising remains a perennial topic of conversation that begins in the weeks leading up to the game and extends for a few days beyond it. In the UK, people generally wait to see what kind of brilliance the team behind the John Lewis Christmas ad has concocted. But these tend to be the exceptions rather than the rule.

In their absence, though, are ideas that have been created in other areas of the marketing ecosystem that have been brilliantly amplified by advertising. In those instances, advertising is no longer playing the primary role in the marketing mix but a secondary, or maybe even a tertiary, role depending on the strength of the central idea.

One example of this dynamic that we have already looked at was Nike's decision to maintain their sponsorship of Colin Kaepernick when the rest of the sports establishment had turned its back on him. It was a brilliantly authentic commitment to the central Nike ethos of supporting the athlete above all else, and it made a major statement about their commitment to their purpose in the face of a sporting culture that was, at best, leaning away from his nonviolent, on-field protest.

That decision was not only authentic to the purpose and principles of Nike, but it also created a massive amount of global conversation—about the brand, about Colin Kaepernick, and, most importantly, about the Black Lives Matter movement. Advertising amplified that cultural moment with a beautiful commercial from Wieden+Kennedy that ended with the line, *Believe in something, even if it means sacrificing everything.*

The fame that results from actions like Nike's support of Colin Kaepernick is not accidental. It's not something that happens by chance to well-intentioned people or brands. On the contrary, fame requires a structured manipulation of the image and of the media to create sensation, celebrity, and celebration. It requires a barrage of energetic activity that injects the brand into the larger cultural conversation. And in paid media, it requires advertising that is created with an earned-first state of mind—one that actively encourages people to engage, to participate—rather than a broadcast state of mind that aggressively urges people to pay attention.

Now, approaching paid media advertising with an earned-first state of mind isn't entirely new. And when it has been done before, it has been used to great effect. In fact, it is quite likely that there is a generation of creative people in the advertising industry that intuitively recognizes that if an idea is good enough to be written about in the *Huffington Post* or viewed on YouTube or shared on social media, then it will work in paid media. And if that generation exists, they likely descend from one man.

Alex Bogusky was the chief creative officer and partner of the storied advertising agency Crispin Porter + Bogusky. The young Bogusky was hired by the already legendary Chuck Porter in the late '80s to jump-start the Miami creative agency Crispin Porter. In 1997, he was made a partner, and through the early 2000s, he and the agency lit a fire under the advertising industry and its standard operating procedures.

The flash point for them came in 1998, when they launched an anti-smoking campaign for the Florida Department of Health. The campaign was called "Truth," and the goal was to establish "Truth" as a brand for brand-conscious teenagers and, in turn, to help them recognize that "Big Tobacco's brand is lies, and our brand is truth." The campaign was highly provocative (particularly for the time), highly engaging, energetic, and youthful. One notable commercial featured a group of teenagers stacking body bags outside Big Tobacco's headquarters.

The media executions were also unusually participatory for the time, including pirate radio activations and fan 'zine production. The media director of the agency commented, *The media component of the campaign is also being developed with suggestions from the teen-age audience…where they tell us they get information, and which media are cool.*[43]

The "Truth" campaign was the precursor to a raft of famous advertising for brands like Mini, IKEA, and Burger King—all of it featuring a signature irreverence from the agency. The beautifully written manifesto of motoring for Mini, delivered as an insert in national newspapers and lifestyle magazines to launch the brand, for example, read:

> LET'S BURN THE MAPS. Let's get lost. Let's turn right when we should turn left. Let's read fewer car ads and more travel ads. Let's not be back in ten minutes. Let's hold out until the next rest stop. Let's eat when hungry. Let's drink

when thirsty. Let's break routines, but not make
a routine of it. LET'S MOTOR.™

(Incidentally, this may have been the precursor to what has
become a standard practice in creative agencies: writing evocative manifestos to present campaigns.) The Mini campaign was
followed by, among other things, the idea to anthropomorphize
a lamp for IKEA—that had us believing the lamp had feelings—
until a presenter reminded us it was just an old lamp and should
be replaced with something newer and better. And one of their
most famous insurgencies, a campaign to promote Burger King's
"Have It Your Way" chicken sandwich that encouraged us to go
online and fire instructions at a man in a chicken suit—moon-
walk, river dance, hop on one leg, and so on.

The creative publicity that CP+B managed to generate,
though not "persuasive" in any traditional way, generated per-
suasively impressive results. Revenues for Burger King between
2004 and 2010 rose from $1.75 billion to $2.5 billion, for example. (Interestingly, the agency was fired in 2011, and by 2015,
revenues had shrunk to $1.1 billion.) And youth smoking rates
declined from 23 percent to 6 percent under their watch.[44]

Crispin was different in many ways from the industry they
operated. For one, they were based in Miami, and there had
never been a Miami-based agency that managed to win and
run national accounts. So, they cut their teeth on work for local
brands—without the budgets that their national-agency competitors enjoyed—which led them to practice their craft in more
progressive ways. And one strikingly simple difference in their
process accounted for much of their creative success.

At the time of their ascent, the broadcast era was still in
full flight, and the creative currency of the industry was the TV

commercial. The "best" agencies were the ones that created the best commercials. The best commercials won the most awards and, at least among people in the industry, were still actively discussed and debated. All creative development in advertising agencies began with the TV commercial—other media executions being considered only when the "winning" commercial had been decided upon.

But Bogusky worked differently. He wouldn't allow his creative teams to present an idea using TV scripts (which was common practice at the time—and still largely is). Instead, he demanded that campaign ideas be presented through the medium of the press release. He was asking, implicitly: How will this idea be communicated when there is no paid media to support it? What is there in this idea that is inherently interesting and worth writing about? And in doing so, he ensured that his advertising campaigns always started with their earned-media execution. And that earned-media publicity would act as a force multiplier for any publicity he generated in paid media. He was entirely earned-first in his thinking and execution.

The work that Bogusky and his agency did inspired a generation of brand builders that followed. International advertising award shows now are full of work that follows a pattern set by CP+B. And campaigns like Dove's Real Beauty continue to demonstrate that multibillion-dollar sales increases can arise from advertising that starts with a premise that will get people talking.

Beyond presenting campaigns with a press release, though (which remains a brilliant and underused litmus test of the strength of an idea), there are four principles that can help ensure that a paid-media campaign can also get talked about.

1. Think 'audience,' not 'consumer.'

2. Determine the earned potential of the idea.
3. Invite media partners to be "in" on the story.
4. Think about earned channels first in production planning.

This is important on several different levels. Theoretically, we know that for a brand to grow market share, it needs to become as widely popular as possible. So any narrowing of the potential audience will work against that goal. Practically, the audience for any brand is almost always bigger than you think.

Take the baby-wipes category, for example. On the surface, the audience would seem obvious: people with babies. But 30 percent of the people who buy baby wipes don't, in fact, have babies. It turns out that baby wipes are particularly good for cleaning the heads of golf clubs. They're also handy to have in the glove box of a car after you've eaten ice cream. They're useful accessories for camping trips. And so on. If a baby-wipes brand limits its view of the audience to people who have babies, it unnecessarily limits its potential to increase popularity and grow market share.

Now, not all those audiences or use cases will warrant paid-media advertising. Some of them will be better served with clever distribution and point-of-sale promotion (in professional stores at golf clubs, for example). But all the audiences should be considered—and any paid-media communication that could reach those secondary audiences should avoid alienating them.

An important shift in mindset happens, too, when you think about audiences rather than consumers. When we think about consumers, we seek to understand how they, yep, consume our products (when they use them, how they use them, why they prefer them over their competitors). That understanding leads to persuasive communications that target those motivations and uses.

When we think about audiences, we tend to think about how to entertain them. We think about what they enjoy watching, what they enjoy talking about, what they enjoy sharing with their friends—and we try to participate in that watching, talking, and sharing in an entertaining and non-intrusive way. We think in terms of earning attention rather than buying it.

This shift to audiences rather than consumers takes us back to the work of Edward Bernays and his focus on the public, not the individual. (And before him, of course, his uncle Sigmund's emphasis on the psychology of the group.) In practical terms, it causes us to look for cultural insights to drive our marketing messages rather than consumer insights, which suggests that we use sociological tools rather than just psychological tools to do so.

There is a whole industry in the paid-media world that uses research to predict the effectiveness of advertising messages. It's been around for decades, and some of the research companies that make up the category have become hugely powerful. All sorts of methodologies and practices are employed to glean insight into whether message A will sell more soap than message B.

Survey research companies ask a barrage of questions about how the advertisement changes attitudes toward the brand—and whether it will increase purchase intention. Qualitative research companies conduct focus groups and in-depth interviews to determine what tweaks could be made to the creative representation that would make it "work even harder." Data and analytics firms run A/B tests of different executions against the same control panel to see which gets clicked more often. And yet, the long-term effectiveness of marketing campaigns continues to decrease.

In full disclosure, I'm a very big fan of research being used in the service of making communications more effective. But in practice, I've found that exploratory research done in preparation for creating the message leads to much more effective work than evaluative research done once the message has been created. And I think there's a central and simple reason for that: all research conducted to determine an advertisement's effectiveness is based on a theory of what makes advertising effective. As we've established, most of those theories—consciously or unconsciously—are anchored by the idea of advertising as persuasion. So, if an advertisement is created to be persuasive, it may test well, but it likely won't work well because that's not the effect that advertising really creates. Conversely, if an advertisement is made with a view to generating creative publicity, it may not test very well, but it may work effectively when (if) it runs.

The simple takeaway here is that for message testing to have any influence on the effectiveness of a paid-media campaign, we should test for the effect we expect to achieve. Clearly, the implication is that we should test creative messages and ideas to see whether they're interesting enough for people to want to talk about them.

As with most things in the marketing and communications world, there are simple ways and complicated ways to achieve that goal. The complicated way would be to create a new testing protocol among a panel of "gen pop" consumers to track the level of discussion and sharing that an idea generates. The simple approach would be to talk to some journalists and influencers about your idea and see whether they think it's interesting enough to write about.

It is slightly astonishing how rarely that is done. Many advertising agencies don't even talk to their colleagues in PR agencies about the ideas they are developing for the brand they all work on.

In fact, probably the greatest insult that can be leveled at a PR professional from a paid-media counterpart is to ask them to "PR this campaign." If the talkability of an idea hasn't been discussed and determined before it's produced, there's very little that even the most skillful PR team can do to make people engage with it. But the opposite is also true. If the talkability of an idea is examined early in the process—by presenting it through the medium of the press release as Alex Bogusky required, involving the PR team, or talking directly to journalists and influencers as part of the development process—then much of the hard work has already been done, and success is much more likely to be achieved.

The idea of virality has been part of the marketing lexicon since 2000, when Malcolm Gladwell published the hugely popular book *The Tipping Point*. The book sought to explain how, aided by the internet, ideas could spread from person to person at astonishing rates, much like the omicron variant of COVID-19 took over the world.

For marketers, the appealing aspect of that viral spread was that it was "free"—in theory, it didn't require paid media to generate creative publicity. My own agency gleefully experimented with the idea of virality for several years, and in practice, we found that ideas didn't spread in the way Gladwell had outlined. There were things that could aid the spread—provocation, youthful energy, and engagement—but on their own, they weren't enough. It was clear to us from a practical perspective that fires needed fuel, and the creative idea itself wasn't fuel enough.

In a more recent book, *Hit Makers* by Derek Thompson, that original idea of virality in marketing is cleverly and articulately dismantled. Thompson confirms what we had seen in practice: things rarely go viral on their own. Instead, ideas need to be supported by what he describes as "diffuse broadcast events" to catch fire. He cites examples like the ALS Ice Bucket Challenge, which appeared to spread through the nominating process on social media (that I'm sure we all fell victim to) but in fact only caught fire after being "broadcast" by Oprah.

In another example he talks about the book *Fifty Shades of Grey*, which was originally published by a small company in Australia to little acclaim. However, it did create enough interest among the fan-fiction community to secure a bigger publishing deal with Random House, and following that, the book was broadcast in quick succession with an article in the *New York Times*, a piece in *Entertainment Weekly*, and segments on *The Today Show* and *Good Morning America*. Following those simultaneous, "diffuse broadcasts," the process of rebroadcasting among smaller groups and individuals created a cultural sensation. (We like to talk about what we know other people are talking about.)

What's important about Thompson's book for marketers and communicators is that it shifts the idea of virality from the theoretical to the practical. Because while we can never know for sure what creative alchemy will make an idea spreadable, we can work to secure the "diffuse broadcasters" that can add fuel to the fire. And the best way to do that is to bring them into the conversation early.

Every brand knows the media and influencers that appeal most to their audience. The truth about the relentless pace of the news cycle today is that all of them are in continuous search for things to write about, talk about, and share. If you take the time to involve them in a conversation about your campaign, stunt, or promotion *before* it has been produced, then you can effectively secure their participation in it. If, for example, you offer to invite a journalist or an influencer to the production itself and give them access to unique content from it, many of them will gladly accept the invitation to participate. In doing so, you have guaranteed the early broadcast events you need to fuel your fire.

One of my favorite examples of determining the earned potential of an idea and bringing journalists in on the story before it was produced comes from the Brooklyn Brothers' London Team for our client Castrol. In absolute terms, it wasn't the most culturally successful thing we had ever done, nor the conversation that engaged the most people, but we were attempting to get people talking about motor oil (not something that naturally engages large audiences), and the fact that we succeeded at all was a triumph.

The pinnacle of Castrol's product line was a fully synthetic oil called Castrol EDGE Titanium. (The "EDGE" in this instance came from its "Fluid Titanium Technology," designed to strengthen the oil and reduce friction in high-performance engines.) The product was undoubtedly brilliant. Castrol is a company that prides itself on technological advancement—its brand platform for many years has been "Liquid Engineering"—but even with that "persuasive" pedigree, it is difficult to get anyone but the most devoted gearheads to talk about engine oil. That was our challenge.

To meet the challenge, we created a campaign platform called the "Titanium Trials," designed as a series of ridiculously complex challenges for professional drivers. One of the most audacious of these trials, called Virtual Drift, was an attempt to have drivers race in what would now be described as the

Metaverse. Two professional racers, in high-performance cars, were put in Oculus Rift virtual reality headsets programmed with a game-rendered racecourse. The cars' physical controls—gas, steering, and gears—were mapped into the virtual world and became game controllers. So, as the drivers maneuvered their vehicles at high speed around an airport runway, in their minds' eye, they were flying around a virtual racecourse.

The idea was intuitively interesting—it hadn't been done before—and it seemed like something people would want to talk about. As we canvassed journalists, influencers, and opinion leaders (covering the media verticals of news, automotive, technology, and gaming), it became clear that the interest was there.

We invited four of those media elites to the filming of the event—each with a different area of interest and angle on what we were doing. The BBC was chosen as the anchor media for news and culture, Jalopnik was invited as our automotive insider, *WIRED* was there to view the technology, and YouTube influencer Austin Evans would relate the gaming aspects of the trial to his 5.2 million followers.

The resulting content was amazing to watch, and each media and influencer outlet had its own unique take on it. In that way, the diffuse broadcast events were secured to launch the trial, followed by a raft of distinct pieces of content distributed more widely across the four media verticals (news, automotive, technology, and gaming), ensuring that, as far as possible, no two outlets would have the same piece of content.

Although the trial was originally conceived as an "earned-only" activation, the resulting content was considered so compelling that it was tested as paid-media content using Castrol's traditional ad-testing methodology. The research was conducted by a large and well-known marketing research company, and although their methodology was known to favor executions that leaned toward the "persuasive," the Titanium Trial (which was pure creative publicity) outperformed their testing norms.

The program was consistently successful for the brand. Virtual Drift, in particular, generated thirty-seven million active views on trackable channels, with over thirty thousand likes and 2,500 comments, and overall generated 1.2 billion impressions across all media outlets. This led our client Vivek Rampal (then global marketing director for the brand) to comment:

"The results speak for themselves. The campaign has not only driven mass awareness for our brand but more importantly it's galvanized consideration and helped drive sales of Castrol EDGE globally."

Everyone is looking for things to talk about, but what will pique their interest most is if they have something of their own to talk about. (This is probably self-evident after looking at how to engage multiple journalists, influencers, and opinion leaders in an idea.) That means production planning for paid-media campaigns should start with a view of how much content will be required to instigate the earned-media conversation.

Traditionally, the TV production process (making the commercials) has been one of the most expensive aspects of paid-media campaigns. As a result, the production itself became a highly choreographed, intensely considered, and carefully controlled process. Storyboards were created to dictate exactly what scenes would be shot and how they would be captured. Lengthy pre-production meetings were scheduled to discuss casting, wardrobe, locations, and props, all with a view to ensuring everyone going into the production had a clear idea of what was expected out of the production. In the traditional sense, the output was generally one, two, or three thirty-second commercials that would be broadcast relentlessly on network and cable TV and streamed in digital video. But that traditional production process doesn't work as effectively in creating the assets required for multiple earned-media outlets as well as their paid-media counterparts.

One simple rule of thumb in thinking about how to create paid-media assets that can also drive earned media conversation is to produce long-form assets before thinking about the short-form edits that will come from them. Thirty-second commercials are usually anchored around a single joke, skit, or piece of action, and a campaign tends to be a collection of three or so similar jokes, skits, or pieces of action. (This issue is magnified further when you think about six-second assets that may be used in digital environments.) However, if a brand enters production with an anticipated output of three pieces of unique content, there simply won't be enough incentive or creative opportunity for outlets to build "ownable," individual stories from it.

An alternative approach is for the brand to approach the production with a view to creating a longer-form piece—a five-minute film rather than three thirty-second commercials, for example. That longer-form film then would include multiple magic moments that could be edited into multiple discrete assets—with the simple addition of a little more B-roll and some deft editing.

This approach has the added benefit of allowing for a complete story to unfold, with fully realized characters and a complete narrative arc. There are very rarely occasions where a full story can be told in a thirty-second commercial. While that isn't a problem in itself, it can lead to creative ideas that don't have much room for growth or development. In that instance, there is a natural halt to the conversation. When it reaches a certain point, there just isn't any further for it to go. When a joke has been told and we've all laughed, we move on. We don't tell the same joke again—or at least not to the same audience.

A real-world example of this type of production planning was done for WaterWipes, a brand of baby wipes launched in 2009 by a relatively small Irish company called Irish Breeze. The brand was created to be the "world's purest baby wipe," and the impetus for its creation was the chronic diaper (nappy) rash that the founder's own baby suffered. As he researched the category, he saw that most products contained surprisingly high levels of chemicals and additives, and he set out to use the expertise he'd gleaned from manufacturing cotton-wool products to create a more natural alternative to what was already available. The result was the WaterWipes brand and its claim to be 99.0 percent water with an added drop of grapefruit seed extract.

Once again, despite an impressively persuasive point of product differentiation, it was hard to engage people in a discussion about the nuances of baby wipes, particularly as the category leaders, Pampers and Huggies, had spent years and many hundreds of millions of dollars establishing their credentials.

To find an entry point into the cultural conversation, the Brooklyn Brothers' team looked at the category and saw a representation of parenthood in both traditional and social media that contrasted drastically with the picture that emerged when we talked to real parents about their experiences. In the media, the picture was perfect. The babies were plump and giggly. The parents were glowing and happy. But that perfect picture didn't represent reality at all. The parents the team spoke to were often unhappy, felt like failures, didn't know what they were doing, and didn't understand why their experience of parenthood didn't match what they saw on Instagram.

The team set out to challenge the media image of parenting with a documentary called *This Is Parenthood*. It was a "vomit and all," real-life look at the experiences of new parents all over the world. The documentary, as a complete piece, was an emotionally beautiful breath of fresh air for parents. From a more rational perspective of marketing efficiency, it not only provided enough editable content to give anchor media partners something unique for their channels, but it also provided the editable assets for a full year of paid-media activation—160 discrete production pieces in all (not including different lengths and sizes of the same piece). And it worked. #ThisIsParenthood made up 75 percent of the entire cultural conversation in the baby-wipes category despite having only a 3.5 percent share of paid-media expenditure. That dominant share of conversation created a 7 percent lift in brand consideration and a 5 percent increase in sales.

Manage Risk, Avoid the Crisis

In traditional marketing and communications organizations, it is still common to hear the brand spoken about in different contexts—the corporate brand, the employer brand, and the consumer brand, for example.

But any marketer or communicator who is trying to build their brand in the Attention Economy recognizes that there is only one brand because there can only be one defining idea. Because of that, progressive communicators build their brand narratives for the corporation, the employer, and the consumer from the same starting point.

Corporate actions or decisions can have a material impact on the consumer and the employee brand. Often, as consumers, we buy from brands that share our values, and we expect brands to play an active role in issues that we care about. (Perhaps more often, we'll avoid brands that stand in contrast to our values.) Sometimes, when brands don't share our values or act in ways that stand counter to the things we believe, consumers will put direct pressure on the corporation. Zara, for example, although having a demonstrably powerful consumer brand, was recently targeted at a corporate level by online activists who were protesting their treatment of Uighur Muslims in apparel factories making Zara's clothes.

Equally, employee actions can directly impact the corporate brand. Frances Haugen, formerly a data scientist at Facebook, created a real crisis for the company by revealing that it had played an active role in disinformation campaigns leading up to the 2016 presidential election and that it actively courted young consumers despite clear knowledge of the mental health issues that social media usage was creating for them.

It is likely not a coincidence that her testimony happened at the beginning of October 2021, and by the beginning of November, Facebook had rebranded at a corporate level to Meta. It may also be connected to the fact that in February 2022, Facebook announced that it had seen its first-ever monthly decline in users, losing half a million users in the fourth quarter of 2021. The actions of an employee had real consequences for the brand at both the corporate and consumer levels.

As Jack Welch would have said, the "naked truth" is that one brand cannot be separated from another. There is only one brand, and in the Attention Economy, the actions of that brand, whether directed at consumers, employees, or shareholders, need to be consistent and true to what the brand stands for.

Given that, it's important now to break down the silos between corporate and communication teams. They need to walk in lockstep, both to benefit from positive synergies in communication and, probably more importantly, to avoid unnecessary crises when better communication and sensible planning could prevent them. This is becoming a particularly pointed issue now that influencer marketing is central to any brand's marketing activity. Vetting potential influencer partners with a clear-eyed view of their potential impact on the brand and on the corporation is becoming essential. Smart communications teams aren't just vetting the influencer themselves—what they write about, what they believe in, controversial stances they take or have taken, and so on—but also vetting that influencer's followers.

Fuel the Fandom

The community of fans who engage with a brand can act as a massive force multiplier for the brand's media efforts. The effect was studied a few years ago by a brilliant and entrepreneurial data analytics company based in New York, which struck a mind-boggling deal with the major digital and social marketing platforms in China to gain direct access to their data on behalf of clients they advised. The company was called Bomoda and was run by Brian Buckwald and Andrew Roth.

The deals they struck gave them access to first-party data from Renren (the Chinese Facebook), Tencent (the Chinese Twitter), and Alibaba (the Chinese Amazon). That access, in turn, gave them unique insight into the way organic social media participation created engagement and how that engagement influenced sales.

One example (that they saw repeated across multiple categories) was for a global luxury goods manufacturer. In the space of a month, the company created and published forty pieces of social content across their platforms. Their partners (primarily paid social-media influencers) created and published another two hundred pieces of content. More interestingly, in reaction to those 240 pieces of "brand-approved" content, the brand's fans who engaged with the story created thirty thousand pieces of user-generated content. Even more impressive, that combination of brand-approved and user-generated content created one hundred thousand overall engagements.

It became clear that user-generated content acted as a force multiplier for "brand-approved" content—that the efforts of users, buyers, and fans of the brand were creating marketplace engagements many times more powerful than the brand could achieve on their own.

There was also a mirroring effect between the brand-approved content and the user-generated content. For example, when the brand featured products that were sophisticated, made from expensive materials, and placed in an upmarket context, the user-generated content also featured products that were sophisticated, made from expensive materials, and placed in an upmarket context. Conversely, when the brand featured whimsical products in fanciful contexts, the user-generated content followed suit.

The brand's own activity had a direct and directional effect on the activity of its fans. (Intuitively, that will feel right to people intimately involved in the creation and management of social-media activity. In many of the best brand social feeds, it is often difficult to distinguish between content coming directly from the brand and content published by its fans.)

The political, cultural, and commercial success stories we examined at the beginning of the book implicitly understand this dynamic. All of them worked tirelessly to inspire their community of fans, but none more so than the K-pop sensation BTS. We touched on the ARMY earlier, but it's worthwhile to look a little deeper to understand the importance of fandoms in the Attention Economy.

The dynamic of the BTS ARMY fandom can be traced back to 1992, when a dance trio called Seo Taiji and Boys built a fan base called the Taiji Mania. Their goal wasn't to simply hang posters of their idols on their bedroom walls and memorize the lyrics to their songs so they could belt them out at the back of the school bus; they were much more commercial in their organization and objectives. The same organized cultural machinery was later employed in the creation of the global BTS ARMY.

One of the most interesting aspects of the ARMY is that there is no central control of their activities and no hierarchy in their structure. Yet, the coordination of their activities is astounding.

Different subgroups find unique ways to express their love for the band. Some go as far as the Chinese ARMY fandom, which bought digital billboards in Times Square to celebrate the fourth anniversary of the band—a media buy that would have run into the tens or possibly hundreds of thousands of dollars. Others provide informal security services for the band when they arrive at venues; small groups will form a security cordon at airports, for example, to keep order and ensure that the larger group of fans doesn't embarrass the band. In a very sweet display of connectedness, not just to the band but to each other, ARMY members also organize themselves into social support groups that gather for study parties, cooking lessons, and other activities.

The importance of engaging with and nurturing the different subgroups that make up the overall fanbase can be traced back to a dynamic first noticed in technology networks. In 2001 computer scientist David Reed published a paper called "The Law of the Pack."

In it, he referenced three types of networks: a one-to-one network, like a telephone system; a one-to-many network, like a TV network; and a many-to-many network, like a social media network.

Reed highlighted that in a many-to-many network, its power increases exponentially with the number of subgroups that form for collaboration and sharing. (So, introducing the community feature on Facebook, for example, made that one-to-one network substantially more powerful and valuable by offering the potential for subgroups to form.)

Once again, this is something that is understood implicitly and acted upon directly by Attention-Economy marketers. Whether it is Donald Trump inspiring the participation of the 3 percenters, the Proud Boys, and the Bikers for Trump to create his base, or BTS uniting the US BTS ARMY and the Chinese ARMY, increasingly, we see that the most powerful brand is the one that most actively nurtures its fans and unifies the greatest number of tribes.

PART FIVE

EVALUATING THE EFFECT

"If they're not talking about you, then
you're not doing your job."

(TIFFANY HADDISH)

ANALYZING TRUTH
AND TALKABILITY

Earlier in the book, we introduced the concept of the Truth and
Talkability Matrix, a simple two-by-two matrix that clearly artic-
ulates the potential for a brand's success or the success of one of
its brand actions. The answer to two simple questions can plot
the brand's position on the matrix: Is it true to the brand? Does
it get people talking?

Truth

Talkability

As with all quadrant charts, the absolute best place to be is the upper-right square: the most truthful activity with the most talkable activations.

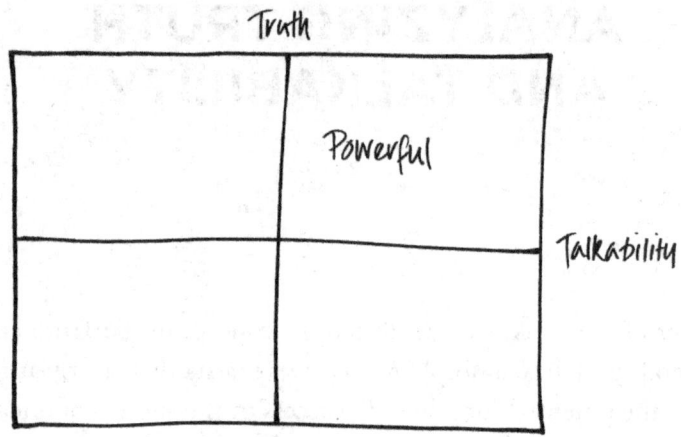

There is little that Tesla does that doesn't fall cleanly into that upper-right quadrant. Their actions are uniformly consistent with their brand's truth of solving great problems and pursuing great dreams and with their personality of swashbuckling invention. Their combination of slightly irreverent provocation with culturally attuned initiatives invariably earns significant media attention.

Take the Cybertruck as an example. Although it has currently fallen from favor, a full-size electric truck feels immediately appropriate for Tesla: pushing the boundaries of electric engines, delivering a product that stands in dramatic contrast to compact electric vehicles like the Nissan Leaf or the Toyota Prius, and focusing on a product category—high-emission trucks—that could make a real environmental impact. A product that could help "accelerate the world's transition to sustainable energy."

Yet Tesla clearly wasn't content with creating an electric replica of old technology. Instead, they designed something that looked starkly new—something that upended our view of what trucks should look like and took more design cues from the Mars Rover than the F-150. And then they called it something new: it wasn't the e-Truck or the iTruck, nor did it reference nature or the past. It looked to the future. It was the *Cybertruck*, damn it! Every aspect of its conception and design was swashbuckling in its innovation.

So, we would expect Tesla's Cybertruck to have earned significant attention and to have generated a lot of conversation and engagement. But how much? How can we measure the effect of Tesla's marketing approach compared to a more traditional alternative?

Well, eleven months after the launch of the Cybertruck came the launch of GM's Hummer EV (electric vehicle). Now that was an idea! A modern reimagining of the vehicle that became the poster child for automotive pollution and was discontinued. An updated but familiar design. A stunning TV commercial with beautiful footage of the truck driving aggressively through desert sand dunes, set to an updated and reimagined version of Led Zeppelin's "Immigrant Song." All of it big, expensive, and rooted in a broadcast-era marketing approach.

So, we have something to measure the launch of the Cybertruck against. And this is what we find.

Analyzing social conversation and media coverage, the Cybertruck dwarfed the Hummer EV in terms of total mentions and total engagements: 565,000 mentions for the Cybertruck versus 11,5000 for the Hummer EV, which is 10.6 million total engagements versus 373,000. The conversational energy is at a completely different level for the two products. Exponentially more people were talking about it. News mentions of the Cybertruck were seven times higher than mentions of the Hummer EV during the launch period. Social mentions acted as a force multiplier and were sixty-seven times higher than social mentions of the Hummer EV. Engagements were force-multiplied again: engagements in both social and news media were exponentially higher for the Cybertruck. What is particularly interesting, though, is the number of unique authors—112,000 for the Cybertruck versus 4,400 for the Hummer EV. Significantly more individuals talking, writing, and posting about one brand versus the other created a dramatically different level of engagement for each. The Cybertruck simply engaged more people in its conversation, which will make the Cybertruck more popular and, we could intuit, ultimately earn it more market share.

So why wasn't the Hummer EV more popular? We can examine that by looking at both dimensions of truth and talkability.

Truth first. The Hummer was a polarizing vehicle. Many people thought it was super cool and badass; others thought it was a symbol of toxic masculinity and climate denial. So, trying to position that brand in a worldview that applauds sustainable energy created cognitive dissonance for prospective buyers. In some part of our brains, the dots weren't joining up; it didn't quite make sense. This was captured in a *Gizmodo* article about the launch that pulled no punches:

> It's clear that GMC is banking on conspicuous consumption as a climate solution. Yet it's that attitude that got us into the climate crisis, and slapping a 1,000-horsepower electric motor in it

is the vehicular embodiment of putting lipstick
on a pig.

So, there were some issues around the authenticity of the product and the role of the Hummer brand.

But what about talkability? Was the conflict between perceptions of gas-guzzling climate denial and progressive automotive manufacturing a tension that could have been leveraged to create real conversation around the launch? Possibly—but that wasn't tried. Here's a sample of the voice-over from the launch commercial: *The real revolutionaries are the ones that can change the game forever... Seeing the world not as it is but how it could be... That's how true greatness is realized. That is how you change the world.*

Now, reread the *Gizmodo* quote. There is something of a disconnect at play. Another significant disconnect arises immediately upon visiting the truck's homepage. The headline statement reads: "The world's first, all-electric supertruck."

Huh? I'm sure there's another all-electric supertruck. Now, maybe there is some competitive nuance that allows the Hummer EV to make that claim. But it's way more nuanced than most readers or buyers would care to examine. (As my client said, "No one gives a shit about 10 percent more chocolate.")

And it was called the EV. (Surely to goodness, someone could have come up with a better name for a truck that was "realizing true greatness" and "changing the world" than the electric vehicle!)

The Hummer launch was an example of broadcast-era marketing: reliance on a controlled message and the expectation that the message could be successfully delivered through paid media. The Cybertruck, on the other hand, was a classic example of

Attention-Economy marketing—the instigation of an uncontrollable idea through earned media. And it worked.

For the sake of illustration—and simplicity once again—let's look at some other examples of campaigns or activations that fall into different quadrants of the chart. Moving from the top right-hand quadrant to the bottom left, we can look at a couple of extremes.

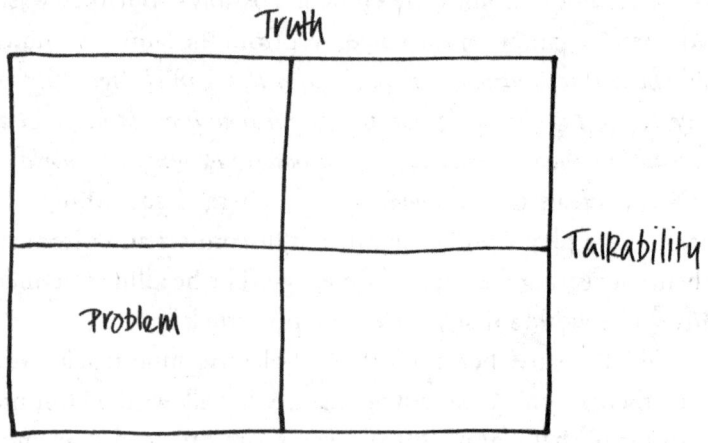

First, picture an influencer activation on social media; in this instance, it is a Valentine's Day–themed influencer post for Listerine mouthwash.

Immediately, we are struck by a barrage of Instagram tropes: an attractive young protagonist waking refreshed to take on the new day, pajamas still on (and yet, curiously, the bed is already made). A "good morning" sign sits atop her nightstand, and her bed is framed by helium love-heart balloons. She's enjoying coffee and is about to tuck into a large stack of crepes with strawberries.

Now, if you're like me in any way, this scene may seem a little contrived or slightly unrealistic. To be open-minded, I'm going to assume there are some folks out there for whom this is a familiar Sunday morning routine. But one thing I can guarantee will not be in the picture—even for those of you who may live this halcyon life—is a bottle of Listerine mouthwash. And yet, in fact, there is a bottle of Listerine mouthwash on her nightstand.

Unfortunately, in a time of rampant paid influencer engagement, this type of communication is all too common. The simple fact that it appears on social media—the perfect forum for honest and real engagement with customers—makes this kind of activation even worse. Harmful even.

Without wishing to flog a dead horse, it is evident that there is not one jot of truth in this post. It doesn't feel authentic to Listerine's purpose—which, as far as I can tell, is to do nothing more than prevent gum disease and bad breath. It certainly doesn't feel authentic to my conception of what Listerine is or does (or where it should be stored).

And it is not talkable. It isn't provocative or exciting in its execution. It doesn't invite the consumer into the conversation (although, to be generous, I would imagine there was a caption that asked, "How do you like to start your morning?"). To state it bluntly, it is an absolute waste of money and effort. One blessing is that it probably didn't cost a lot of money.

Something in the bottom-left quadrant that did cost a lot of money, however, is Chevrolet's sponsorship of the Manchester United soccer (football) jersey.

In 2018, Chevrolet paid $64 million for the naming rights on the jersey. The price was up 34 percent from 2017.

Now, to begin by being generous, Manchester United has a staggeringly large fan base. The numbers may be debated, but according to research from global research company Kantar, in 2012, they had 659 million fans globally, with about half in the Asia Pacific region and a quarter(ish) in the Middle East and Africa. Those are huge numbers. One in ten people around the world. So, on the surface, you could argue that paying ten cents per person to reach a massive global audience thirty-eight times every season (assuming they watched at least part of every game) is pretty good value. And being generous again, Chevrolet did have a stated goal of increasing market share in Asia Pacific at the time of the sponsorship, so perhaps you could argue that this was a financially prudent move. But they would be broadcast-era arguments—based on the assumption that a controlled message (in this instance, the display of a logo) through a massive paid medium would have a positive brand-building effect. It didn't.

Although the number of potential impressions for the season was high—31.3 billion—the engagement from fans was very low: 76,000 social mentions and 766,000 total engagements. So, we go from paying ten cents per person to reach them thirty-eight times to eighty-three cents for every time one of those people actually engaged with the "message," and an engagement here could be as simple as a like. At the same time, Chevrolet's market share in Asia Pacific was going in the wrong direction: down, not up.

So, what went wrong? Simply put, Chevrolet paid for impressions and gave no thought to how they would create engagement. It was an example of broadcast-era marketing rather than earned-media marketing. The sponsorship did not feel true to the Chevrolet brand. Now, Chevrolet's brand purpose is not immediately apparent, but you can glean from their website that they view themselves as "a 100-year-old practice of protection, caring for others and evolving technology." Manchester United does not immediately come to mind in connection with that goal, nor does it align with consumer perceptions of Chevrolet. The Chevrolet brand isn't sold in the UK under the Chevrolet name—cars are badged as Vauxhall there. So, there was no authentic connection to English football. And there was no active engagement in the communication. It was a passive display of branding: no invitation to participate, no excitement, no provocation. It ticked all the broadcast-era boxes: It was consistent in its use of distinctive brand assets, and a big new logo on the front of their heroes' jerseys was unlikely to go unnoticed by fans. It sought to reach prospective buyers and refresh brand-linked mnemonics. But all for naught. In fact, it may have been counterproductive.

Interestingly, and as a bit of an aside, if this had been a General Motors sponsorship done in service of their ambition of moving toward an all-electric future, perhaps the authenticity and engagement would have been easier to build. The future of transport is a topic that may be more present in the Asia Pacific than anywhere else in the world. And it wouldn't have taken much to find an engaging link between an electric future and electric play on the field. But I digress. That didn't happen.

Let's jump upstairs now to the top left-hand quadrant: high authenticity and low engagement. An interesting example here is Pantene.

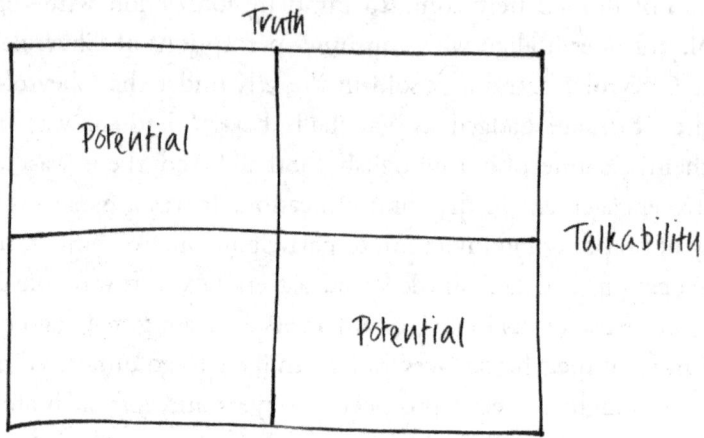

Pantene, of course, is a hair care brand, created seventy years ago after an accidental discovery that Pro-Vitamin B5 directly contributed to stronger hair. As a brand, however, its role stretches beyond the product benefit of hair to what great hair can do. It elegantly states its truth as having "the Power to Transform." And it bases that narrative on the idea that "hair impacts every person on the planet. Some may dismiss it as trivial, or superficial, but the reality is, hair has the potential to change our day and perhaps even our world."

At the end of 2019, Pantene partnered with the Dresscode Project to launch a transgender visibility campaign. The Dresscode Project aims to find and create hair salons and barber shops where trans and non-binary people can feel safe and welcome, and Pantene conducted a study that found 93 percent of people who identified as trans or non-binary had been misgendered while at a salon.

To publicize the partnership and the mission, Pantene launched a video called "The Power of Hair" that featured a number of trans and non-binary activists. The brand offered to make a donation to the Dresscode Project every time the film was shared.

The project is entirely consistent with Pantene's brand truth. The film is beautiful—full of intimate and inspiring stories, elegantly filmed and edited with a wonderful soundtrack. But unfortunately, it wasn't talkable. The video was structured more like a broadcast commercial than an earned-first communication. The narrative arc was complete. The film ends with the title, "Whatever hair you dream of, we stand with you." A wonderful commitment, but neither requiring nor asking for any participation. There was no hook, no involvement for the audience. And, unfortunately, it didn't engage people. Of the sixteen thousand total brand mentions for Pantene during the campaign launch period, the campaign only received four hundred of those mentions.

Now, we've already dealt with the issue of attribution, so it may well be that Pantene was mentioned positively because of the campaign, even though the campaign itself wasn't mentioned. But even if that were the case, the objective of connecting donations to shares of the video was not met. (One year later, the video had received fewer than eleven thousand views on YouTube.)

So, onto the bottom right-hand quadrant, where activities are highly engaging—inviting, exciting, and culturally relevant—but don't feel true to the brand. They don't connect to its purpose or to consumers' perceptions of it.

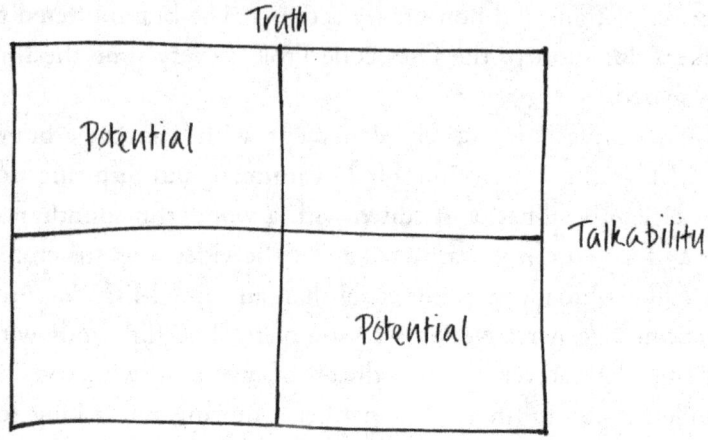

Now, examples in this quadrant are likely to be the most contentious. Many of the examples that jump to mind first do so for a very good reason: they are truly talkable. But the question has to be asked: did they actually have an impact on the brand or the business of the company? So, just to throw the cat among the pigeons, I'm going to use a highly lauded example of modern creativity: Volvo Life Paint.

For any of you who haven't heard of Life Paint, it was a collaboration between a Swedish company called Albedo 100 and Volvo Cars UK. The paint was a reflective spray originally developed to be applied to the antlers of reindeer to make them visible to drivers at night (a particularly thoughtful innovation).

In 2015, though, it became very famous (in the advertising world, at least) when a UK advertising agency rebranded it as Volvo Life Paint and positioned the product as something that could save the lives of city cyclists. A video of the product was made, and two thousand cans were offered for sale at Volvo dealerships in London. The idea caught fire quickly. The cans sold out immediately, another twenty thousand were ordered, and the video was viewed 130 million times (without paid advertising support). The campaign was awarded the highest honors in the advertising and communications world, winning both a Cannes Lions Grand Prix for creativity and an Effie Award for marketing effectiveness.

So, there's no doubt that the Life Paint idea was talkable (particularly for the budget that was allocated to it, which was quite small). But was it true to the Volvo brand? Did it actually improve the brand's standing in the world?

On one level—the simplest—you could argue that it was. Volvo as a brand has been known for safety for decades. The company invented the three-point seat belt in 1959, and, in an impressive show of altruism, waived its patent rights so other manufacturers could use the invention to save lives. They invented the rear-facing child seat. They were the first automotive manufacturer to implement side-impact airbags. Volvo's safety credentials are impressive and perhaps unparalleled. And Life Paint is a product that aims to keep people safe at night. So, at one level, the connection is clear.

On another level though the connection is a little tenuous. Firstly, Life Paint is a product for cyclists, and Volvo doesn't make bicycles. Not that the company doesn't care about the safety of cyclists. In fact, in 2008, they introduced their City Safety System, which allowed vehicles to slow down or stop autonomously if they sensed a collision was imminent. The system could detect cyclists, pedestrians, and animals. So, they'd put real engineering muscle into technology that could prevent accidents involving cyclists. Did they need to supplement that with a product that cyclists would use themselves to increase their nighttime visibility? Probably not.

One of the go-to destinations for reviews of cycling products is BikeRadar. Their reviews are well respected, written by real cyclists, and cover every aspect of the sport. Their review of Life Paint was poor: *A well-intended product, but sadly an ineffective and gimmicky one too. Buy if you're unwilling to wear anything hi-vis and don't mind throwing money at a disappointing alternative.*

The big difference between reindeer and cyclists (one of them, at least) is that cyclists can wear reflective clothing and reindeer can't. So, a product that was brilliantly "well-intentioned" in its original form does come off as a bit gimmicky when there are simple and widely available alternatives to help you be seen in the dark.

One must imagine that a "gimmicky" safety innovation felt like a sword to the heart of Volvo's safety engineers, which would explain why the product was never commercialized. According to a *Hypebeast* article about the campaign, when Life Paint was revealed in 2015, "Volvo, alongside its Swedish start-up partner, Albedo 100, decided that they would amp up distribution if the product receives a ton of fanfare."

On the surface, that seems like an entirely reasonable—even smart—commercialization strategy: gauge interest in the product first, and if enough interest is generated, then move into production and distribution. In this instance, though, the supply-chain consideration seems to have been an afterthought. The product was never commercialized. But did the campaign improve any brand metrics? An article in *The Drum* referencing the campaign's many awards stated:

Saving cyclists' lives is an altruistic motive, particularly for a car brand, but the reality is the
campaign and more importantly the approach
need to be able to shift hard brand metrics. It is
why Grey's planners and strategists are exploring
ways to measure the impact ideas like Life Paint
have and how Volvo can scale them up should
they prove successful.

The article was written over a year after the launch of the
campaign, and the agency's strategists were only then "exploring"
ways to determine its brand effect. Again, it feels like a bit of
an afterthought. The final nail in the coffin of truth came later
when *a video campaign promoting Volvo's Life Paint product—a
hi-vis spray paint designed to help cyclists stand out in dark conditions—has been canned by the Advertising Standards Authority
almost two years after its initial launch.* It was deemed that the initial
promotional video for the product had been a little overzealous
in its demonstration of efficacy, which is a shame. A wonderfully
engaging idea ended up being a stunt with little authentic connection to the brand.

FANNING FLAMES AND PUTTING OUT FIRES

In each of these quadrants, there are things that can be done to improve the efficacy of the campaign. Starting in the top left, for example:

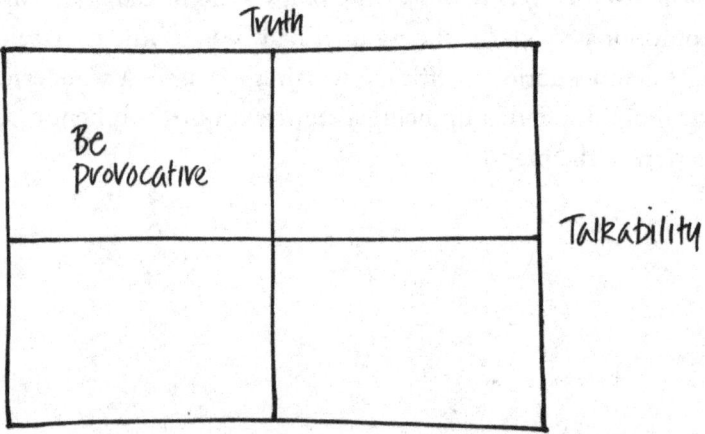

A lot of broadcast-era advertising and communications falls into this bucket. These are "quiet" messages in a controlled environment. Now, if the message is, in fact, true to the brand, and if the branding of the communication is clear and effective, and if there is paid-media support behind the message, it can build on the communications that have come before it to create a bank of goodwill toward the brand. Brand concepts will be reinforced. And that is no bad thing. It is, however, an expensive thing—and a slow thing.

To enjoy the force-multiplier effect of an Attention-Economy communication, the brand would have to do something more talkable—more provocative and more inviting. It would need to shift from passive to active in its communication.

Demonstrations outside famous hair salons, for example. Something that could be talked about and written about. Something that has a chance of disrupting the news cycle to some degree.

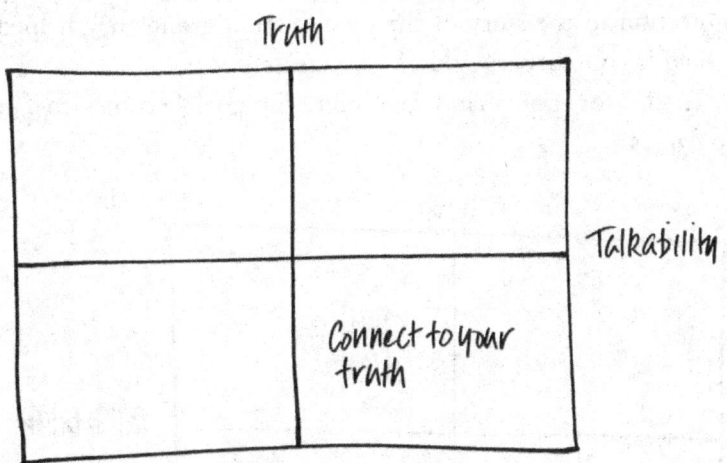

The activities that fall into the bottom right-hand quadrant follow the form of the traditional PR stunt: something that grabs attention but is forgotten quickly. (The kind of thing, perhaps, that Bernays excelled at—talkable but not entirely true to the brand.) The goal here is to make it memorable by connecting the activity more authentically to the brand's truth and consumers' perceptions of it.

Volvo, for example, is certainly perceived as a car you buy when your primary focus is safety. But the brand's truth is anchored by the Swedish word *omtanke*, which means caring or thoughtfulness.

Perhaps the Life Paint activation could have been more authentic if it had been connected to Volvo's sustainability plat-form and they donated the paint to conservation groups around the world to keep animals safe near roads at night (the original purpose of the product). Perhaps Volvo drivers could have given back by sponsoring the donation of a can of paint when they bought a car; by doing so, they would be given an ongoing connection to the story of the conservation group they helped through a content series that Volvo created.

In the top right-hand quadrant, the goal becomes to fan the flames.

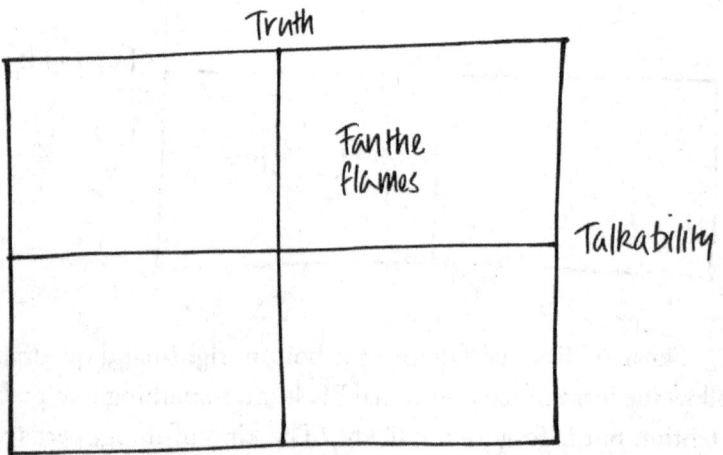

If the activity was earned-only rather than earned-first, consider supporting it with a paid media buy. If it was a social media activity, think about how a structured media-relations effort could support the story. If it was PR- and media-relations-led, think about the social extensions of the idea.

And, at the same time, think about how to give the idea longevity. How can it be extended? How can it stay relevant and exciting? Can it be revisited after a period of time? (Like the production-design reveal of the Cybertruck a year after its initial unveiling, for example.)

In the bottom left-hand quadrant, the advice becomes simpler.

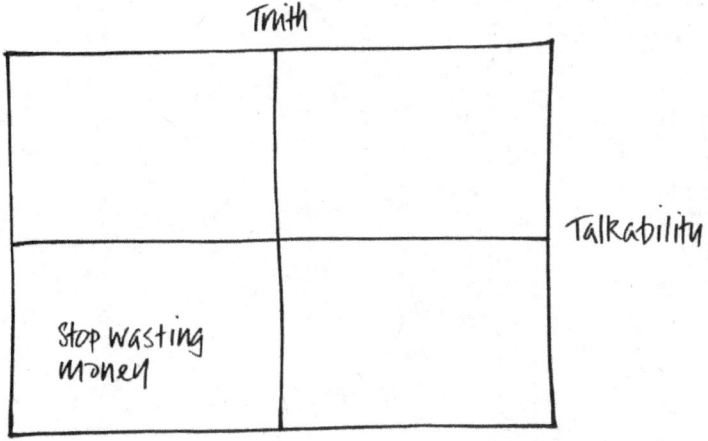

Don't do it. Rethink your sponsorship contracts. Rethink your communications mix. Maybe even rethink the agency you work with or the structure of your internal creative team. There is an alarming amount of bottom-left communication in the world, and it is just noise. In fact, you could go further and say that it is cultural pollution. It is the plastic supermarket shopping bag floating limply in the river of popular culture. It doesn't help the brand, and it certainly doesn't help the consumer. Overall, the need here is to help your team understand the benefit of truth and talkability in their work.

CLOSING THOUGHTS

The practice of building brands by focusing on owned, earned, and shared media rather than paid media isn't new. Ray Kroc, a notorious showman, used it to great effect to build the McDonald's brand, as did Howard Schultz for Starbucks and Richard Branson for Virgin. But it wasn't until Web 1.0—and the Attention Economy it spawned—that a new approach to marketing became a truly viable path to brand building at scale (at least in the absence of a charismatic or enigmatic leader like those above). And it wasn't until the rise of Web 2.0 that this approach gained wide adoption, becoming the modus operandi of the unicorn brands that emerged during that era.

And here we are, on the verge (or precipice) of another technological leap—AI and Web 3.0. Roy Amara would remind us that with these, as with all new technologies, we are likely to overestimate the effect of the technology in the short term and underestimate the effect in the long run. And there has certainly been no lack of "new paradigm" puffery during the first blush of this new technology. But equally, there is an almost certain truth that there will be long-term applications that we can't even imagine now as we explore the slightly clunky and disconnected present. Another certain truth is that technology moves ever faster, and computers become ever more powerful, so it will take less time to get to the long-term realization of AI and Web 3.0 than it did to get to that point for Web 2.0—and less time still to get to that same level of actualization than it did for Web 1.0. What's almost certain, too, is that just as the marketing principles of the Attention Economy were more useful and usable in Web 2.0 than in Web 1.0, they will become more important still in Web 3.0.

The ability to broadcast controlled messages in a world where digital and physical realities merge is difficult to imagine. If it's easy for us to avoid advertising messages now when we're consuming digital media, it will be materially easier to do so in the future. And brands will need to get more comfortable with the need to earn the attention of the consumer rather than trying to buy it.

The implications for the marketer are clear. For every experiment they conduct with generative AI, minting tokens or building storefronts in virtual worlds, they should be conducting parallel experiments on how to put greater emphasis on the owned, earned, and shared disciplines and how to put more truth and talkability into all their marketing.

And if they do, they may find that they become one of the political, cultural, or commercial successes that define the next technological generation.

ENDNOTES

1   Jason Lynch, "$1.2 Billion and Counting: How NBCUniversal Secured Its Biggest Olympics Advertising Windfall Ever," *Adweek*, August 4, 2016, https://www.adweek.com/convergent-tv/12-billion-and-counting-how-nbcuniversal-secured-its-biggest-olympics-advertising-windfall-ever-172697/.

2   Rob Salkowitz, "How Much Streaming Can We Take? New Data Sheds Light on the OTT Revolution," *Forbes*, April 10, 2019, https://www.forbes.com/sites/robsalkowitz/2019/04/10/how-much-streaming-can-we-take-new-data-sheds-light-on-the-ott-revolution/#45693d116407.

3   Daniel Frankel, "Quarter of OTT Users Say They Have Too Many Subscription Services," *Multichannel News*, May 23, 2019, https://www.multichannel.com/news/ott-market-not-saturated-hub-research-says.

4   Guy Debord, *The Society of the Spectacle*, trans. Donald Nicholson-Smith (New York: Zone Books, 1995).

5   Herbert A Simon, *Designing Organizations for an Information-rich World* (Baltimore: *The Johns Hopkins Press*, 1971), 40–41.

6   Charlie Warzel, "I Talked to the Cassandra of the Internet Age," *New York Times*, February 4, 2021, https://www.nytimes.com/2021/02/04/opinion/michael-goldhaber-internet.html%20Attention%20is%20power.

7   Bob Garfield, "The Chaos Scenario," *Ad Age*, April 13, 2005, https://adage.com/article/viewpoint/bob-garfield-s-chaos-scenario/45561/.

8   Marisa Meltzer, "How Emily Weiss's Glossier Grew From Millennial Catnip to Billion-Dollar Juggernaut," *Vanity Fair*, October 10, 2019, https://www.vanityfair.com/style/2019/10/how-emily-weiss-grew-glossier-from-millennial-catnip-to-billion-dollar-juggernaut.

9   Rebecca Nicholson, "Glossier founder Emily Weiss: 'Beauty has very little to do with looks,'" *The Guardian,* December 29, 2019, https://www.theguardian.com/global/2019/dec/29/glossier-cult-beauty-brand-founder-interview.

[10] Jonathan Bacon, "Marketing in the Age of Trump," *MarketingWeek*, October 4, 2016, https://www.marketingweek.com/marketing-in-the-age-of-trump/.

[11] Nicholas Confessore and Karen Yourish, "$2 Billion Worth of Free Media for Donald Trump," *New York Times*, March 15, 2016, https://www.nytimes.com/2016/03/16/upshot/measuring-donald-trumps-mammoth-advantage-in-free-media.html.

[12] Shannon Carroll, "BTS is back. Here's how it will grow the global economy and South Korea's GDP," *Quartz*, June 13, 2025, https://qz.com/bts-reunion-kpop-group-army-hybe.

[13] Raisa Bruner, "The Mastermind Behind BTS Opens Up About Making a K-Pop Juggernaut," *Time*, October 8, 2019, https://time.com/5681494/bts-bang-si-hyuk-interview/.

[14] Kim Parker and Ruth Igielnik, "On the Cusp of Adulthood and Facing an Uncertain Future: What We Know about Gen Z So Far," Pew Research Center, May 14, 2020, https://www.pewresearch.org/social-trends/2020/05/14/on-the-cusp-of-adulthood-and-facing-an-uncertain-future-what-we-know-about-gen-z-so-far/.

[15] LM Foong, "'The ARMY Still holds the power': Inside the organized chaos of the BTS fandom," Medium, DeconRecon.asia, July 31, 2019, https://medium.com/@deconreconasia/the-army-still-holds-the-power-inside-the-organised-chaos-of-the-bts-fandom-9a54f4864ef2.

[16] Noah Brier, "Why is this interesting? – The 2x2 Edition," Substack, Why Is This Interesting?, August 12, 2020, https://whyisthisinteresting.substack.com/p/why-is-this-interesting-the-2x2-edition.

[17] Mark Ritson, "Interbrand's 'iconic moves' invite ridicule for the discipline of branding," *MarketingWeek*, October 25, 2019, https://www.marketingweek.com/mark-ritson-interbrand-iconic-moves-ridicule-branding/.

[18] Byron Sharp, *How Brands Grow: What Marketers Don't Know* (Oxford: Oxford University Press, 2010).

[19] Philip Kotler, et al., *Marketing Management*, 16th ed. (London: Pearson, 2022).

[20] Jacob Jacoby and Robert W. Chestnut, *Brand Loyalty, Measurement and Management* (New York: John Wiley & Sons, 1978).

[21] Ingrid Lunden, "Amazon Music passes 55M customers, still lags behind Spotify and Apple," *TechCrunch*, January 22, 2020, https://techcrunch.com/2020/01/22/amazon-music-passes-55m-customers-across-its-free-and-paid-tiers-but-still-lags-behind-spotify-and-apple/.

[22] Sarah Vizard, "Adidas: We over-invested in digital advertising," *MarketingWeek*, October 17, 2019, https://www.marketingweek.com/adidas-marketing-effectiveness/.

[23] Byron Sharp, "Mental availability is not awareness, brand salience is not awareness," Personal blog, March 26, 2011, https://byronsharp.wordpress.com/2011/03/26/mental-availability-is-not-awareness-brand-salience-is-not-awareness/.

[24] Marvin Minsky, *The Society of Mind* (New York: Simon & Schuster, 1988).

25 Robert Heath, *The Hidden Power of Advertising* (Lincolnwood, IL: NTC Publishing, 2001).

26 Phil Knight, *Shoe Dog: A Memoir by the Creator of Nike* (New York: Scribner, 2016).

27 Émile Durkheim, *The Elementary Forms of Religious Life* [1912], trans. Karen E. Fields (New York: Free Press, 1995).

28 Al Ries and Jack Trout, *Positioning: The Battle for Your Mind* (Columbus, OH: McGraw Hill, 2000).

29 Lorne Buchman, "The untold story of how Apple built a retail empire on trial and error," *Fast Company*, October 14, 2021, https://www.fastcompany.com/90686027/the-untold-story-of-how-apple-built-a-retail-empire-on-trial-and-error.

30 Reema Khrais and Maria Hollenhorst, "The creative force behind a viral corporate TikTok account," *Marketplace*, January 17, 2022, https://www.marketplace.org/story/2022/01/17/the-creative-force-behind-a-viral-corporate-tiktok-account.

31 Andrew Ehrenberg et al., "Brand Advertising as Creative Publicity," *Journal of Advertising Research* vol. 4, no 42 (July 2002): http://dx.doi.org/10.2501/JAR-42-4-7-18.

32 Jenni Romaniuk and Byron Sharp, "Brand Salience and Customer Defection in Subscription Markets," *Journal of Marketing Management*, vol. 19 (February 2003): 25–44.

33 Paul Feldwick, *The Anatomy of Humbug: How to Think Differently About Advertising* (Leicestershire, UK: Troubador Publishing, 2015).

34 Brad Adgate, "Agencies Agree: 2021 Was a Record Year for Ad Spending, With More Growth Expected in 2022," *Forbes*, December 8, 2021, https://www.forbes.com/sites/bradadgate/2021/12/08/agencies-agree-2021-was-a-record-year-for-ad-spending-with-more-growth-expected-in-2022/?sh=57eeee577bc6.

35 Claude C. Hopkins, *Scientific Advertising* [1923] (Scotts Valley, CA: CreateSpace Independent Publishing, 2010).

36 Edward L. Bernays, *Crystallizing Public Opinion* (New York: Dover Publications, 2019).

37 R. Reeves, *Reality in Advertising* [1961] (Widener Classics, 2015).

38 Paul Feldwick, *Why Does the Pedlar Sing?* (Leicestershire, UK: Troubadour Publishing, 2021).

39 Sigmund Freud, *Group Psychology and the Analysis of the Ego* [1921], trans. James Strachey (New York: W. W. Norton & Co., 1990).

40 Bernays, *Crystallizing Public Opinion*.

41 Edward L. Bernays, *Propaganda* (New York: Liveright Publishing Corporation, 1928).

[42] "Nike Nearly Dropped Colin Kaepernick Before Embracing Him," *New York Times*, September 26, 2018, https://www.nytimes.com/2018/09/26/sports/nike-colin-kaepernick.html.

[43] Stuart Elliott, "The Media Business: Advertising; Crispin Porter & Bogusky coordinates Florida's anti-smoking campaign by and for teen-agers," *New York Times*, April 14, 1998, https://www.nytimes.com/1998/04/14/business/media-business-advertising-crispin-porter-bogusky-coordinates-floridas-anti.html.

[44] Statista, "Revenue of Burger King worldwide from 2004 to 2022," June 27, 2025, https://www.statista.com/statistics/266462/burger-king-revenue/.

ACKNOWLEDGMENTS

I should start by thanking Anthony Fauci. If I hadn't been stuck at my dining room table for twelve months, I would never have forced my ADD into a corner for long enough to attempt a project like this. But also, damn you, Anthony, for forcing me to attempt a project like this.

My pals at Golin, particularly Matt Neale and the leadership team who keep work fun and make it exciting to think bigger.

Early readers George Bryant, Stuart Hazlewood, and Jackie Stevenson were a blessing for their patience and critique. Joe Mandese for giving me an outlet to develop my thinking—twice.

Michael Fanuele, Stephen Waddington, and Amelia Appel who helped me understand the world of publishing. Debra Englander and Lauren Campbell at Post Hill Press who helped me navigate that world.

My talented brother-in-law Carl Knapper for his illustrations.

Dawn, and the Langeland plan, that got me off my ass to push this over the line.

My family, who in an impressive show of fortitude, resilience, and support, managed to feign interest in my slightly abstract topic across conversations that spanned months, and in some instances years.

But most especially for Amanda, who makes me believe I can do things that I otherwise wouldn't do.

ABOUT THE AUTHOR

Paul Parton is the group chief strategy officer for the Golin Group, overseeing the research, brand planning, and data and analytics functions across four agency brands. He came to Golin via its acquisition of the Brooklyn Brothers, the creative agency he co-founded in 2005. Under his leadership, that agency grew from six people in an artist's studio in Chelsea Market, New York City, to 120 people across three countries, serving clients such as Pepsi, NBC, Jaguar Land Rover, and Rémy Martin. He began his career in the "University of Advertising" as a graduate trainee with Ogilvy & Mather. He writes a monthly column for *MediaPost* that focuses on the changing nature of media consumption, particularly the impact of social media on brand building. He has lectured on brand planning, strategy, research and insights, and modern marketing at Fordham University, Iona College, the University of Rhode Island, and Roger Williams University. He holds an MBA with distinction in strategic marketing from the University of Hull.